Manufacturing Mastery

Manufacturing Mastery

The Path to Building Successful and Enduring Manufacturing Businesses

Rebecca Morgan

Routledge
Taylor & Francis Group

A PRODUCTIVITY PRESS BOOK

First published 2021
by Routledge
600 Broken Sound Parkway #300, Boca Raton FL, 33487

and by Routledge
2 Park Square, Milton Park, Abingdon, Oxon, OX14 4RN

Routledge is an imprint of the Taylor & Francis Group, an informa business

© 2021 Taylor & Francis

ISBN: 9780367691196 (hbk)
ISBN: 9780367691165 (pbk)
ISBN: 9781003140481 (ebk)

Typeset in Garamond
by Deanta Global Publishing Services, Chennai, India

To JJ

Who never lets the clouds keep me from seeing the sun

Contents

Acknowledgments

No one writes a book without the help of others. Even great novelists have family, friends, teachers, and life experiences created with too many to mention. This book, while written entirely by me, benefits from my many teachers along the way. With over forty years in manufacturing, the list of individuals impacting my thinking is voluminous. I will acknowledge several of them here and apologize to the many more I fail to mention.

My volunteer work with the Association for Manufacturing Excellence (AME) and Association for Supply Chain Management (APICS, ASCM) provided introductions to great thinkers while providing experiences I could not have otherwise had. Among the willing are Doc Hall, David Mann, Gary Stewart, Mark Lewis, Greg Bruns, Ellen Sieminski, and Steve Chapman. My professional development work with Alan Weiss has connected me with some of the finest consultants the world has to offer. Noah Fleming, Rob Oddi, Colleen Francis, Chad Barr, and Jody Irving are just a few of the contributors to my growth. Their willingness to share and challenge thinking is incredible. I am indebted to these and many more.

Clients have provided insights, great questions and challenges, and the laboratories in which I learned. Idelle Wolf, Vince Nardy, Jim Bluhm, Ned Sherry, and Joe Pullella are a few of the leaders with whom I had fun while helping their companies progress. Non-clients who have been willing to share their thoughts, successes and failures include Sanjay Singh, Marc Braun, John Kramer, Frank Koentgen, and Joanne Deys.

Alan Weiss inspired me to share my thinking with leaders of manufacturing businesses through this book and taught me the process of writing a powerful proposal for commercial publication. Joe Pullella provided helpful critique of the initial table of contents, resulting in improved logical flow. Greg Bruns and Sanjay Singh read early drafts of the manuscript and made suggestions that significantly bettered the final product. Sharon

Holmes provided creative ideas and skills in developing graphics verifying that, in fact, a picture is worth a thousand words. And my dear friend Ellen Sieminski provided editing skills and laughter that prove that what doesn't kill us makes us stronger. I can only hope to thank these contributors enough, while absolving them of responsibility for any errors. Those are all mine.

Two people kept me going during the process. Aviv Ben-Yosef is my accountability partner, who was writing a book at the same time. His energetic confidence and fast progress propelled me forward daily. Lastly, I want to thank my partner, Jim Juknialis, without whom my consulting career may not have begun all those years ago. His belief in me then, during this writing experience, and all the years in between, is forever cherished.

About the Author

Rebecca Morgan, President of Fulcrum ConsultingWorks Inc. in Cleveland, OH, has not only helped others do it; she's done it herself. She served as an operations executive in large manufacturing organizations for fourteen years prior to starting her consulting business in 1990. A prolific thinker and writer, Becky's consulting and advisory help manufacturing leaders develop dramatic capabilities to create and deliver amazing value to their constituents. Additionally, her published writings, podcasts, and speeches prepare executives to address strategic opportunities and challenges.

Ms. Morgan has BA and MS degrees in economics and additional postgraduate education. She is certified as Fellow by The Association for Supply Chain Management (APICS/ASCM) and was awarded lifetime member status of the Association of Manufacturing Excellence (AME). In addition, she is board approved in Operations Management by the Society for Advancement of Consulting and was inducted into the Million Dollar Consultant® Hall of Fame in 2017, then one of only seventy-five consultants in the world to be so honored.

She continues to advise leaders of mid-size manufacturing businesses ($100MM–$1B), serve on both non-profit and for-profit boards, contribute to the body of knowledge, and support media efforts to inform the audience about issues important to manufacturing businesses.

While accomplishing all that, Becky always makes time for sports, motorcycle riding, and world-wide travel. She has experienced more airplane take-offs than landings. Think about that one.

Introduction

This book encapsulates learnings from an improbable journey, not yet complete. The third child of a small-town postmaster and a grain trader for Cargill, I fell in love with manufacturing the first time I saw it. The choreography of information, tangible things, people, and communication immediately attracted me.

I already had degrees in economics and through those was exposed to two fundamental concepts, one of which is absolutely true, the other of which is demonstrably false. The former is scarcity; the latter the rational man. Both suppositions are impactful in building a successful and enduring manufacturing business.

If all resources were plentiful forever, and humans behaved intellectually, manufacturing would be simple. But they aren't, they don't, and it's not. Leading a manufacturing business is tough.

Formal education emphasizes strict capitalism and its unparalleled ability to generate wealth. The school of hard knocks offers different lessons. Attend any MBA program and the accounting professors will teach you how to record financial transactions–real and imagined–while marketing professors teach you how to convince the world it needs what you offer. You will be instructed in theories about strategy, operations, and finance. And then you hit the real world of manufacturing.

Soon you will reach a critical decision point. For some "soon" is immediately, for others it can be a few decades. But when you're there you will know it. Either accept all you were taught and execute it as best you can or ask yourself if that's all there is.

I once thought mission and vision were useless fluff. I was wrong. I used to think that my job as a corporate executive was to maximize profits. I was wrong. Every manufacturer has five equally important constituencies: investors, customers, suppliers, employees, and the community at large which includes the future. We cannot ignore, or take advantage of, any of them. Being in business simply to generate the most money for a select group of investors is boring and short sighted. In reality, maximizing current profits will cost future profits. But the tombstone will say "they made some people a lot of money."

So, what does that mean for the leader of a manufacturing company? It means they need to understand the distinction between a financially successful business and an enduring one. Of course, an enduring business needs profits to fund its future, but there is an important difference between accounting profits and strategic profits. The former is calculated and reported as required and distributed as seems to make sense at the time; the latter is both earned by building the capabilities and relationships that endurance requires and invested in pursuing a mission and vision that matters.

As you read this book, you may well scoff at much of what I declare mandatory. Isn't a profitable product enough? The answer depends on your intentions. If you simply want to feed your family and little more, this book may be interesting but irrelevant. A business that meets that very viable intention is successful; it will not be enduring. If success to you means increasing sales or keeping it going another year, judge your efforts by those metrics.

If instead, you want to build a successful and enduring manufacturing business, this book provides guidance for you. Focus on developing an organization that will accomplish its mission while improving the lives of many along the way is distinctly different from the focus on current wealth and the exit plan. There are textbooks aplenty for the latter. I focus on the former because I believe it is a worthwhile use of my intellect and life, and yours, and the earth's limited resources.

Manufacturing Mastery: The Path to Building Successful and Enduring Manufacturing Businesses presents steps in a logical sequence, but probably not in prioritized progression for your company. Assuming your organization already exists, you and your team may have mastered some sections and never considered others. I have included an assessment tool as an appendix to help you determine your current strengths and opportunities to use in making priority decisions most appropriate for your situation.

This book begins with the fundamentals. Chapter 1 addresses why increasing effectiveness of meaningful change is a requirement for manufacturers of all shapes and sizes; it also explains the importance of living the need for change. Chapter 2 considers mission, vision, and core values, as well as their required role in building an enduring business. Those are the equivalent of "do not pass go; do not collect $200" for this process.

Chapters 3 through 9 provide a dynamic guide for the manufacturing leader who wants to neuter ambiguity and overwhelm, and develop a realistic, progressive, and responsive thinking process that enables success and endurance. They describe a business operating system framework that is the foundation for connecting the many pieces of a manufacturing business into an effective, profitable operation. The reader will walk through the elements, relationships, capabilities, and mutability twenty-first-century manufacturing requires. Executives of manufacturing companies will be better able to think about and execute viable strategies, leveraging changing socioeconomics while accomplishing the mission. Chapter 10 integrates it all. With it and the baseline assessment tool in the appendix you can take that first critical step: grasp reality. By seeing where you currently are compared to where you want to be, you can begin to identify steps to move forward.

In many situations, leaders must be explorers. That takes courage. It also takes differentiating what is known that we can count on, what is unknown that we must discover, and what is known and unknown that really isn't all that important right now. While no book can realistically provide step-by-step instructions for your individual business, this one shows you the landscape and explains what to look for and how best to explore and progress. It will help you get through the storms, sun, sideswipes, and alluring successes. As Chapter 4 makes abundantly clear, you are not alone in this. Don't act like you are.

The bad news is that none of this is the silver bullet you may have been hoping for. Everything explained here takes work, thinking, practice, learning, change, and focus. The good news is that the work is much more fun and interesting than is simply maximizing profits. It creates meaning rather than tries to discover it. When you pass the baton to the next person who will lead the organization ever closer to accomplishing the mission, you will be able to admire the ground that has been covered, the value delivered to many, and if it matters to you, your contribution to building a successful and enduring manufacturing business.

Businesses that endure focus on ensuring the future, not on building a bigger today. Perhaps that distinction is why so few manufacturing businesses stand the test of time. With the help of this book, you can build one that does.

Chapter 1

The Manufacturing Metamorphosis Imperative

Unaddressed Can Kill Your Business

The CEO of a closely held manufacturing company recently told me that his team simply cannot make meaningful change any faster than they have been, and he believes that is true for his suppliers, competitors, and customers as well. If he is right, that supply chain is in trouble. If only he believes that, his business is in trouble.

Our world is increasingly dynamic. Perceptions of how the world works that underlie assumptions in business are evolving and disappearing. We assume that children go to school, as young adults they go to work, and when mature adults they retire. For demographic, socioeconomic, and life expectancy reasons, that will not remain true.

Education must be ongoing. Call it retraining if you'd like, but continually creating and building new knowledge and skills is required. There is no profession, whether menial or elevated, that will remain unchanged over a decade. Paid work will be part of life after the now-current retirement age and will not be confined to minimum-wage, low-skill roles.

Yes, women are still the only ones who can have babies, but men increasingly want to share in raising them. Both have an interest in investing time in the process. Consumers increasingly care about the mission of a business and how actions impact the world. Layer on top of those long-term trends fluctuating trade agreements and tariffs, tax rates, and laws, and you easily see why significant change is inevitable.

No business can ignore the new reality. It is the role of leadership to prevent people from believing they are immune. You can learn to make meaningful change faster than you have in the past—if you want to. But as George Carlin said, "Ya gotta wanna."

Why All Manufacturers Must Change

"This has worked for years" is a common refrain. As a business and operating strategy, it is now suicidal. Small companies do not get a pass; they are as impacted by our changing reality as any other business. They often have less room for error than their larger brethren. A manufacturer reluctantly incorporating new value-adding thinking and capabilities could slow, but not prevent, its demise. Innovation in materials, products, and processes is rapidly changing our world and doesn't care about your comfort or ability to respond. That may sound harsh, but it is true.

This is a sampling of innovations, most begun over ten years ago, that are now routine.

- Virtual, assisted, augmented, and mixed reality (VR/AR/MR)
- Robots that can walk, run, open and close doors, and go up or down steps
- Smartwatches
- Drones
- Artificial intelligence (AI)
- CRISPR genome editing
- Digital payment systems such as Square, Zelle, Venmo, Apple Wallet, or even bitcoin
- Smartphones with high-quality cameras
- High-precision GPS
- Additive manufacturing (3D printing) objects from the size of the eye of a needle to a large building, using materials as varied as bio, metal, ceramic, and carbon fibers

In each case, the initial discovery or development did not immediately change our lives, but as they became more reliable, flexible, and affordable, they did. For example, few manufacturers had an additive manufacturing strategy in 2010, despite the fact that the technology was about thirty years old. In the last decade 3D printing capabilities exploded. Today, we cannot ignore its role in our present or future. The same is true for VR, AR, MR, AI, and, of course, the umbrella concept of Industry 4.0. The evolution of each listed innovation continues, along with the thousands that aren't listed. Our capabilities, strategies, and tactics must continue to evolve as well. Stagnant is not an option.

Expectations of all those around us have changed as well, and even more quickly. Meeting customer assumptions used to be easy. Ship them as many line items in approximately the right quantities as close to the requested date as made sense to you. The concept of deviations was developed to address out-of-spec conditions that the customer probably could use anyway. We trained the customer to understand just how hard our jobs were and to carry inventory as a cushion. Those days are gone.

Customers now expect user-controlled pull (e.g., more Americans now have streaming services than cable television to access on-demand shows, rather than live by the providers' schedules), location-independence (e.g., telehealth, Carvana, or the ability to customize package drop-off/pick-up locations), and same-day delivery (e.g., Amazon Prime or grocery stores). People don't categorize their expectations by our degree of difficulty; they simply want what they want, when they want it, where they want it. Sounds reasonable. It's our job as manufacturers to figure out how to provide that to our markets.

Because of all this, manufacturing is changing along with the rest of the world. It has to. The pace required for developing important capabilities is picking up and will not slow down. People don't expect less, nor will they. While there are those who say manufacturing is dying, it is not and will not. Short of a universal vow of poverty, growing economies and an expanding middle class will only increase demand. While manufacturing will not die, individual manufacturing companies will if they do not learn to thrive in this new world. Operations has to step forward.

Think of your company's differentiating value-adding characteristics on a horizontal scale of one to five, five being best on earth. Now think of that entire scale as always sliding to the right. Maintaining your current score requires improvement at the rate the scale is moving. Improving your relative competitive position requires even faster—or, likely, breakthrough—improvement. The faster the scale moves to the right, which, if you're not the one defining world-class, is governed by enhanced expectations and performance of others, the more quickly you must improve the value you deliver to not fall off the left side into the annals of history (Figure 1.1).

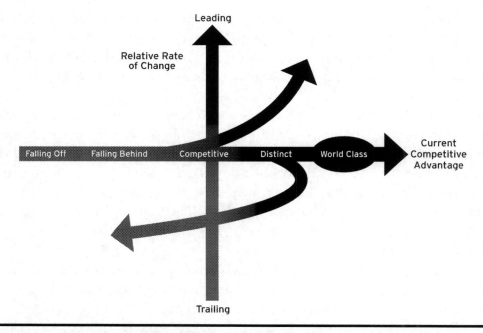

Figure 1.1   The Manufacturing Metamorphosis Imperative

So how must a manufacturer be able to change not only to succeed, but to endure? The sliding scale metaphor demonstrates that you have to successfully change in ways that matter to the market minimally at the development rate of others. That's simply to not lose ground to those who currently deliver more effective value than you do; the path to hanging on for now. Both factory-as-a-service (FaaS) and product-as-a-service (PaaS) are changing not only what manufacturers sell, but how they think about business models. We have to get better at what matters.

Lean and Continuous Improvement

Continuous improvement (CI), a concept considered the gold standard for advancing value a decade ago, can now be outpaced by advances in design and technology. The breakthroughs enabled by those developments can create step-function increases or entire revolutions in delivered value. No manufacturer can afford to ignore those factors.

We have all heard the metaphors of the lion and the gazelle, and the bear chasing a person. We know that to eat, the lion has to be faster than the slowest gazelle, and to remain alive, the gazelle must be faster than the fastest lion. We know the person doesn't have to run faster than the pursuing bear, but only faster than his companions. Those metaphors are instructive in some cases, but not in building an enduring manufacturing business.

Why not? The market evolves as a much hungrier animal than those menaces. We must not only clear the fastest-moving threat, but also be able to fend off new challenges from other beasts. That is why both speed and agility matter. But they, too, are insufficient. We must profitably create and deliver amazing value to the market and not simply provide more of the same, faster.

Think of Moore's Law. It was the prediction of a very smart man with an understanding of physics. The law referred to a rate of progress that should and could happen with integrated circuit development. Not unlike President Kennedy's proclamation that within a decade the United States would put a man on the moon and return him safely home, Gordon Moore had no idea how it would be done. Each man believed his manifesto possible, and each was proven right. Moore's Law may have run its course, although Intel argues it has not. What will be technology's next invigorating force? It does not rest on its laurels. The best is yet to come. It is those levels of expectations and technical cooperation that manufacturing must emulate.

Certainly, there are truisms to consider. People can fear change they do not control. Denial is a natural human resistance to massive change. Right now, you may be denying that accelerating both speed and agility, while developing and delivering new value, is a requirement of your business. We frequently fail to recognize our own potential, as well as that of others. Each of those and much more will be overcome while building "one giant leap for mankind" capabilities.

What does this mean for lean manufacturing? Lean is an American term created initially to describe variations of the Toyota Production System (TPS), but it has little standard understanding. To some it is a euphemism for staff reductions; to others it is a set of tools for continuous improvement (CI) that is rarely continuous. Let's take lean at its best and consider it respect for the whole person.

Embedded respect for people is a requirement of all enduring organizations, but, alone, is insufficient. First, note that as good as Toyota is, it is not the best operating manufacturer in the world. More importantly, that company does not rely on its production system to create its enduring future. Its effective processes of CI throughout the business enable it to be successful now. That the system develops skills to create and implement rapid change should not be minimized in considering the future. It is important to remember that it has mission, vision, and core values that underlie everything.

Great design trumps any CI methodology. So, too, can a superior understanding of human behavior and needs. Advances in technology—coupled with powerful strategic thinking—will propel manufacturers past those with a reliance on lean, because together they enable acceleration that matters.

None of this is to say that lean is wrong or bad. All means of continuous improvement are valuable in making an existing manufacturing operation successful. The compound value of those changes is profound. Toyota's respect for people is a core value that underlies its every strategic and tactical decision. It is also foundational to the TPS improvement process; the company proudly claims it builds people who build vehicles. By focusing on developing critical skills in its employee and supplier base as it pursues an important mission, it is, in fact, building endurance. Don't confuse the tools of lean with what really needs to happen.

If your organization does not demonstrate rapid improvement as a core competency, it is time to make that a priority. Luckily, you're not in this alone. Businesses that endure will coordinate with and leverage all five of their constituencies (investors, customers, suppliers, employees, and the entire community at large). With lived vision, mission, and core values that energize each participant, the potential is indeed amazing. Without them, a manufacturer may suffer from Delusional Excellence®: believing it is better than facts confirm.

Determining Your Speed of Change

I have long advised clients that together we will identify and implement new strategic capabilities as quickly as they can handle. One of those strategic capabilities is always the ability to effectively create and integrate value-adding change more and more rapidly. Why would any business choose to improve its competitive position more slowly than it could? Changing faster than it can risks breaking the company. As leaders we must master walking that fine line as we advance it.

What does *breaking* look like?

In the 1990s, Toyota decided to significantly expand its geographic footprint and number of operations. Unfortunately, it did so faster than it could effectively embed its business operating system, extraordinary design thinking, and expectations of working toward perfection in the new operations. That growth-oriented decision diluted those critical aspects of the company's success worldwide. Its internal process performance standards effectively fell. Quality problems arose and other challenges, though less obvious to the customer, continue. *Breaking* doesn't have to mean close up shop, but it certainly means a turn for the worse.

My partner had a heart procedure at the number-one-ranked heart hospital in the world during COVID-19. I was not allowed inside with him, being forced by the hospital's safety rules to meet him outside when he was released. Providing verbal going-home instructions to someone still affected by anesthesia was not a good rule, but it didn't *have* to fail totally. Unfortunately, it did.

The printed going-home instructions did not match what the doctor had told me right after the procedure, nor did they match my partner's physical condition when he was released. Small suction cups attached to his torso remained; the staff had forgotten to remove those. Also overlooked was applying the portable, temporary monitor the doctor had ordered, and providing instructions for it. Two weeks filled with calls and electronic messaging passed before we had the appropriate monitoring equipment and required information.

While the actual medical procedure was *not* broken, the release process was. Going-home instructions verbalized to someone influenced by anesthesia and not matched with equipment or the doctor's communication provides one example of broken. In response to changing understanding of COVID-19 and related regulations, the hospital system had been modifying too many processes and responsibilities too quickly for the staff to adequately handle. The heavy workload on support staff, coupled with related attendance and reassignment challenges, no doubt contributed to the failure.

Breaking may appear gradually, or all at once. The critical point is that leadership prevent it when possible, and recognize and fix it when prevention fails.

During that pandemic, businesses in every industry pushed the boundaries of how quickly needed changes could be effectively determined, communicated, implemented, and verified. Certainly, not every organization or every process broke. Some companies had to quickly decide how to handle unexpected excess capacity, facing ambiguity about future volumes. Others had to dramatically increase throughput while maintaining all standards. The abilities to quickly and effectively make those adjustments were developed in advance; those without that level of agility experienced much more difficulty in reacting well. "What if?" is not an empty question.

While some businesses and organizations were breaking, others discovered they could implement significant changes much more quickly than previously believed. Dyson developed a new ventilator in one month. Film location scouts helped New York City identify and secure temporary hospital locations in days instead of months. Manufacturers rearranged equipment and changed shift schedules within days, while facing upheaval in supply, demand, and employee availability. Many of those same companies shifted gears entirely to produce health-care-related personal protective equipment (PPE).

New products, new scheduling techniques, new cooperative agreements, and, of course, new massive work-from-home (WFH) capabilities were implemented. It wasn't always pretty, but it was done. Waiting for perfection is like waiting for Godot.

New evidence suggests that leadership sometimes had held the reins of change too tightly. As those reins fell, we saw creative thinking break through prior restraints. Suppression had taken many forms. Unspoken, but common, limiting assumptions included: "We can't work with them! They are our competitors." Complacency often limited potential: "We make widgets, not those things." Vision over imaginary walls had been blocked: "We work with the entertainment industry, not medical."

Now that we've proven it, we cannot ignore what we know we can accomplish. None of us can afford that. Perhaps we needed extreme pressure to see what was possible. The pandemic gave us that, as world wars and a president's audacious proclamation had previously.

Reacting with an on/off mindset—changing everything or changing nothing—fails without exception. Go fast, but not too fast. It is the leader's responsibility to ensure that the organization responds smoothly to the requirements of change. At any point, an organization has a maximum rate of healthy velocity and then acceleration. To prevent breaking, leaders must establish a governor to ensure it is not exceeded. As the organization gains agility, the cap increases, and the business changes to reach the new capability. Finding that sweet spot is a requisite skill for leaders to constantly build and adapt.

Impact on Leading Today

As a practical matter, the awareness of the step-function changes required of enduring manufacturing businesses impacts how we lead them today. As you read this, your organization likely offers some competitive advantage to your market. That strength will be irrelevant sooner than later.

The most amazing ability to effectively incorporate change in a business with poor strategy or no viable mission is wasting energy. The organization will be agile but changing for no sustainable reason. No single competency will ensure the endurance of a business. Lack of critical capabilities will preclude endurance. As leaders, we must constantly identify those compulsory requirements if we are to remain relevant. How do we do that?

Every manufacturer has metrics lovingly called key performance indicators (KPIs). Despite the adjective "key," it seems "the more, the merrier" for all too many organizations. Financial numbers often dominate. They are lagging indicators that measure effects, rather than cause. Leading indicators that reflect cause to drive action and improve decisions are less common and sadly lacking from most executive dashboards. Whether on white boards, electronic screens, or monthly reports, KPIs that reflect performance against targets mean nothing if the targets are irrelevant or do not reflect a solid strategic path. It is easy to lull one's self to sleep.

Learning which corners to take, which velocity to change, or how best to pass the competition is cultivated by looking forward and outward, while understanding the strength and limitations of the vehicle you captain. Experience—that is, accumulated knowledge and skills—bolstered by cognizance of current and expected conditions, along with a clear vision, can be leveraged to identify the optimal course. That is why intimately integrating strategy with the five constituencies mentioned earlier is also a requirement of endurance and must be reflected in metrics. The expertise is the enterprise.

Lasting companies maintain focus on accomplishing their mission and vision and living their core values. They do not look for a case for change; they live it. Those organizations concentrate on a different kind of profits—strategic profits. An enduring company focuses not on maximizing current profits, but rather on leveraging those profits to better reach its mission and vision in alignment with its core values. Profit maximization interferes with forever. Earning, saving, and investing of strategic profits facilitate forever.

THE MANUFACTURING METAMORPHOSIS: FINAL THOUGHTS

■ Metamorphosis is a struggle between now and the future; the future always wins.

■ While manufacturing will not die, individual manufacturing companies will if they do not learn to thrive in our evolving world.

■ Profit maximization interferes with forever. Earning, saving, and investing of strategic profits facilitate endurance of your business.

If your organization is intimidated by the requirements of accelerating improvement, your personal, demonstrable openness to learning and calm guidance through ambiguity will make an important difference.

Chapter 2

If Vision, Mission, and Core Values Don't Anchor Your Business, What Does?

"More" doesn't excite the troops

If maximizing current profits does not guarantee an enduring business, why do so many leaders focus there? They are not stupid, nor destructive in most cases, so what are they thinking? We know that top-executive compensation at publicly held companies includes incentives to maximize stock value. Those values usually rise with increasing profits. The individuals on the board of directors, who set those compensation schemes, are not stupid nor destructive either. So why do they reinforce near-term thinking?

Primarily because most of them think that is their job. There is good reason for them to believe that.

The Birth of the Profit Maximization Expectation

In September of 1970, leading economist Milton Friedman wrote an article published by *The New York Times* that has had an overwhelming impact on business in America. His motivation was a Ralph-Nader-led organization applying pressure on General Motors (GM) to add directors to "serve the public interest." Nader's Campaign GM presented several resolutions to be voted on by shareholders, each of which was subsequently defeated.

General Motors decided to take a few small steps in that direction to quiet the criticism.

Friedman, repeating what he had written in his 1962 book *Capitalism and Freedom,* insisted that in a free enterprise economy, the prime responsibility of corporate leadership is satisfying the goals of its owners, the stockholders. Anything other than that would be irresponsible, and even worse, "pure and unadulterated socialism."

Underlying Friedman's argument were two points: firstly, that the social good is the responsibility of government and its taxes and not of allocation decisions by individual corporate executives, and secondly, the assumption that shareholders' primary interest is maximizing their return on investment, best accomplished by maximized profits. He suggested that any stockholders preferring social investment over maximized returns were, by definition, encouraging the company to "tax" the money of strictly financial investors to favor specific social preferences without agreement. While his book was primarily read by economists, Friedman's *New York Times* article became widely known and referenced.

In a nation of laws, of course there have been disputes addressing the role of stock price in business decision-making. Corporate law seems clear that in certain situations stock price is to be maximized and given priority over other investment sources. There doesn't appear to be a single law requiring that operational decision-making target stock price or profit maximization, but more a collection of laws and court decisions that encourage investor primacy over the personal preferences of internal management.

Personal financial incentive, coupled with accepted legal interpretation and a common commercial belief that maximizing profits is the duty of corporate leaders, explains why many leaders of manufacturing businesses focus on maximizing profits.

Nonetheless, many choose otherwise, although not without critics.

The Purpose of the Corporation

Paul Polman was named CEO of Unilever in 2009. He quickly began to make major changes to the global consumer products company. He announced that the business would no longer provide quarterly guidance to financial analysts, telling the investment world that he would not be focused on short-term profitability. He emphasized long-term intentions to make the company socially and environmentally responsible. The CEO acquired brands aligned with his thinking and rejected a takeover bid from a company with very different values. While many attacked his leadership, share price and financial results were strong.

Mr. Polman stepped down in 2019, replaced by Alan Jope. Mr. Jope has said, "I intend to build further on Unilever's century-old commitment to responsible business. It is not about putting purpose ahead of profits, it is purpose that drives profits."[1] While long committed to ethical behavior, and like many, not blemish-free in that regard, the strong focus on stakeholders over shareholders is still relatively young at Unilever. It can provide a solid foundation for ensuring Unilever endures as the board and leadership remain steadfast in that business philosophy.

Barry-Wehmiller is a 130-year-old manufacturer, now over $3 billion in sales. The current CEO and majority owner, Bob Chapman, took the reins when his father died suddenly in 1975. The troubled business immediately faced financial ruin, but young Chapman pulled them through. Now well known for his book and Truly Human Leadership model, the CEO didn't begin the cultural transformation of Barry-Wehmiller until more than twenty-five years into his role. Few cultural transformations are overnight successes, and this one was no different. The belief system is now well ingrained throughout the entire business of over 11,000 employees. The company's statement *"We measure our success by the way we touch the lives of others"*[2] likely sounds strange to a numbers-oriented manufacturing leader, but the financial results reflect validity of the mission.

Numerous manufacturing companies in addition to the two mentioned above seek endurance through a purpose other than to make more money for investors. To find examples of the much larger group that focus on near-term success, hoping endurance will take care of itself, look to those listed on public stock exchanges. The vast majority of those names fall into this category. But change is in the air.

On August 19, 2019, the pendulum was given a strong push in the direction of focus on all stakeholders, rather than solely shareholders. That day, the Business Roundtable—a collection of CEOs of top companies in the United States representing a broad swath of industries who together provide advice on policy issues to impact the economy—shared a formal statement totally rebuking Milton Friedman's view of the purpose of a corporation. Friedman was, of course, not mentioned, but the message was clear. Signed by over 220 CEOs, the "Statement on the Purpose of a Corporation" declared a commitment to provide value to all five constituencies for "the future of all our companies, our communities, and our country."

It seems they understand that maximizing current profits is not the path to an enduring business. Again, time will tell how this statement impacts behavior and decision-making in those and other organizations, but at least those looking for permission to consider all constituencies have received it.

As leaders acknowledge that profits and purpose are inextricably linked, they are beginning to reflect the priorities of the global populace. What we value as humans is impacted by memorable events. In the United States, the Great Depression, Pearl Harbor, the 1968 My Lai Massacre, John Kennedy's and John Lennon's assassinations, the 9/11 attacks, and the election of the country's first black president were defining moments. Much of that is irrelevant to the rest of the world where citizens are impacted by equally significant, but more local, events.

All people in all countries are impacted by the more gradual and more life-altering potential of global warming, globalization and the immediate communication and sharing of ideas it enables, advancing and widespread technology, and visibility into the increasing divide between the haves and the have-nots. It is now easy to see inequities, learn from advancing science, and change personal focus from fighting for food, clothing, and shelter to improving the quality of life for all.

Young people, who outnumber those aged fifty and above,[3] do not like what they see, and are demanding better. Globally, those generations are leading awareness and change. Despite significant progress in many arenas, governments and religious organizations have not prevented these problems. We are in this together and look for leaders of an influential sector to step up. None of us wants a legacy of declining living conditions for our children.

Call it desperation if you like. Widely shared concerns have created global demand that business repair the problems and reduce the inequities it is viewed as having created. The widening spread[4] between executive and employee compensation has grabbed attention. CEO compensation in excess of 200 times that of workers is common and growing. Stock compensation typically contributes to much of that disparity, but base pay is frequently greater by factors of ten or more. Add to that the historically unsafe working conditions in manufacturing coupled with negative environmental impacts—some through ignorance and some through malice—and increased outsourcing to poorer countries that continue those practices, and it becomes obvious why business is in the spotlight. Especially your manufacturing business.

The Distinction between Success and Endurance

Fair or not, the consumer base expects business leaders to care about something other than making more money today. Furthermore, if you want to build an enduring organization, a firmly held belief about what truly matters must be defined. Only with that can you make and execute a commitment to invest strategic profits in improving the quality of life both now and in the future. Ongoing debates about climate change and inequality provide two examples of why individual businesses cannot wait for general consensus to act. You and your business are at an inflection point. This is the time to transform from a Mr. Hyde reputation into a permanent Dr. Jekyll. A negatively viewed company cannot endure.

A leader has to create and maintain the respect of all stakeholders to build a lasting future. A manufacturing business is typically given the benefit of the doubt at least initially, perceived as faithful to its mission, vision, and core values. If those claims are valued by your constituents, the question becomes how the promises are verified by actual conduct. As transparency increases, whether through blockchain or other technologies or by public promise, consumers can make informed choices on something other than price. And they will.

This is where the distinction between successful and enduring begins.

Documented mission and vision statements became common in the mid-1970s when Peter Drucker introduced his theory of business management. Discussion of terms like purpose, vision, mission, and strategy often muddy, rather than clarify, the distinctions. I encourage you to accept the definitions used in this book while you read it. There is no benefit to letting perceived semantics interfere.

I will use *mission* as the reason why your business exists. *Vision* is a description of what that will look like as it is accomplished. *Core values* are the truths that your business will live by in the entirety of its behavior. *Strategy* is the chosen path to fulfill the vision. *Purpose* is the foundation for all.

A significant number of mid-size manufacturers have statements of mission, vision, and core values. A surprisingly small group shares those convictions broadly through their websites. Why keep such important information a secret if you want the active support of each constituent group? It's easy to find general statements of services provided and industries served, making *selling* the most visible mission. While frequently describing how nice and caring they are, few trumpet a vision or mission beyond themselves.

For example, "to be the best metal stamper…" speaks to *what* you do, not *why* you do it. The comment refers to a company's targeted future, no one else's. It reflects current production capabilities and materials in existing markets. That goal limits agility by building a high fence around what is and what is not acceptable. The intention may well be important for current sales, but it does little to build a lasting future.

Purpose does not have to be world-changing, and should not be quixotic. A metal stamper might consider "provide neighborhood residents with safe, high-paying jobs that develop and deliver value to our customers" if that fits the true intention of ownership. Consider how that could enhance an organization's future.

One very large company describes a vision to be one of the most nimble and innovative consumer packaged goods companies. This is similar to the claim of the metal stamper, with "best" defined as nimble and innovative. The words are admirable, but can they anchor endurance? Can they attract optimal engagement by each constituency to the team? Do they make us believe that they care about anything as much as they do profits?

A more captivating vision is "we will end death on the job by 2050," supporting the mission of "Preserving human life on, above, and below the Earth."[5] That purpose can attract the active involvement of prime representatives of each constituency. The most talented or least expensive is less important than the potential contribution to creating a stronger team. Because every manufacturing business requires the help of its constituencies, focusing on value that matters to them as well as yourself is a requirement of building endurance.

One successful manufacturer[6] describes its mission as "restore glory and dignity to manufacturing." Its vision is along the lines of "better indoor working environments for hard-working people." The organization speaks openly about commitment to four of the constituencies. A family-owned business, it chooses not to mention investors.

Communicating purpose is where things get interesting. The owner clearly states his purpose: "We exist to glorify God by enriching the quality of every life we touch." Business operations appear to consider that a small "g" to support any religious beliefs, including atheism. The owner's statement merely claims a purpose "higher than ourselves." Looking beyond one's own self-interest is increasingly attractive worldwide.

The company does not know if that purpose statement has unintentionally excluded potential investors, customers, suppliers, job applicants, or community support. The important point is that any such exclusion is not by intention. It would reflect self-selection by any who object to God as part of the owner's purpose. Leadership and employees mutually commit to the whole person, not just job skills. Expectations are high, and so is support to grow and learn. The culture is one of gratitude expressed daily, unconditional love, and behaving with care and integrity. An atheist, Muslim, Buddhist, or LGBTQ individual could appreciate that environment.

Your company vision, mission, and core values do not have to appeal to everyone externally. You're trying to build an enduring company, not please everyone all the time. The guiding standards claimed must be central to all behaviors and decision-making within the business and build, attract, and retain capabilities the mission and vision require. In doing so, honesty is always the best policy.

Your Five Constituencies

Long-term relevance requires capable investors, customers, suppliers, employees, and community support. An organization viewed as merely trying to make more money will struggle to attract and retain those critical partners. Even for many investors, a purpose larger than money has to be at the forefront.

Let's take a minute to consider the five major constituencies of any manufacturing business and the integral role each has to your success building an enduring company (Figure 2.1).

Investors

The investor constituency is not limited to stockholders, though every business has at least one of those. In publicly traded stock instances, actual stockholders change from minute to minute. While some institutional and individual investors think longer term, day traders care only about making money on stock price variations. One segment of shareholders may focus strictly on dividends they expect to receive. Others consider perceived risk profiles as they try to manage the risk-return exposure of their overall portfolio. Private-equity firms typically concentrate on growing and selling a business within a few years to create a cash return on investment (ROI) for their investors. Some choose to become longer-term operators.

There are other equally important potential sources of funds for your business. While banks and various financial institutions are concerned with

Figure 2.1   The Five Constituencies of Every Manufacturer

safety and payback of their investment, many also care about your role
in the community. Their trust in you is paramount to their willingness to
extend financing. Your manufacturing operations may serve primarily as a
means to an end as they seek to grow their deposit base. Family and closely
held private investors typically take a longer view of success, but not always.
I've witnessed arguments in many such groups in which the demands of
one are not consistent with the passions and thinking of the others.

As you can see, the investor constituency is not a homogeneous group.
There is no reason to assume that maximizing company profits is the prime
concern of all investors. Businesses do have an obligation to make priorities
clear with investors. Choosing Benefit Corporation legal status in the United
States or becoming B Corp certified by the third-party, nonprofit B-Lab
broadcasts a company commitment of service to multiple stakeholders. The
tenets of Conscious Capitalism, a principles-based framework implemented
by companies such as Google, Starbucks, Whole Foods, and Costco, highlight consideration of all stakeholders for a higher purpose. Those formal
commitments are not required to enable purpose beyond profits, despite Mr.
Friedman's beliefs. But some transparent communication of organizational

intention is vital in serving investor needs as they serve yours. You will need that group, even if you do not ever borrow money. Their future matters to yours.

Customers

The customer or marketplace is another constituency of your business. Without them there is no future. But the proclamation that the customer is always right is a fallacy. We have to deliver what they perceive to be value, but we are also obligated to create value for the future they don't yet envision. Whether it is Henry Ford's "they would have asked for a faster horse" or the "computer on every desk and in every home" of Bill Gates, most enduring businesses are in front of solving problems the market may not yet acknowledge.

If you don't improve the condition of your customer, why should they continue to do business with you? Every manufacturer knows that *what, when,* and *how many* are mere ante. Most who claim quality as their differentiator do so because they don't know what else to say. Reliable, predictable, and repeatable performance in responding to customer request does not set a high bar.

It is a responsibility to improve the quality of life for customers. Reducing frustration, simplification of complexities, and sharing important insights are general descriptions for what many manufacturers provide. Whether you support the space exploration business, the corner grocery store, or an individual consumer, those and more apply. It does you no good to believe you are in the widget business. Instead, realize that endurance requires vision that attracts passion. As President Kennedy demonstrated, you will discover *how* along the way. Always remember, you are not alone in that endeavor.

The real differentiator is the market seeing you as integral to its enduring future. That view does not rely on today's technical capabilities, but rather on attitude, exploration and sharing, and true partnering to develop expertise in anticipating and addressing opportunities. Google—a self-declared Conscious Capitalism adherent—and Facebook want my data; Apple is committed to maintaining my privacy. Which am I more likely to trust with my future? Good intentions and business model can sometimes be at odds, but not forever. Increased transparency by Google and Facebook could make a big difference in their ability to endure.

Suppliers

Every manufacturer has important suppliers. Suppliers not only keep their promises, they make you better. Vendors sell hotdogs. Suppliers bring expertise and ideas, share experiences and observations, and engage deeply in enhancing the value of your products and services. As one of your critical constituencies, the supply base is respected partners, or it is a herd of vendors. As the COVID-19 pandemic taught us, even toilet paper and cleaning supplies benefit from a relationship based on mutual respect and support.

Why would a supplier choose to work with you, to commit to your success, if you use them to unilaterally improve your cash flow and hurt theirs? Why would a business expend energy on improving your competitive position if you are not committed to helping theirs? Supplier assessments that focus on traditional delivery metrics are of limited value to anyone. Effective supplier evaluations are bidirectional and focus on building mutually important capabilities.

Offloading accountability for compliance with labor and environmental laws to suppliers is merely moving the pea to a different walnut shell. Responsibility cannot be outsourced. Shared values and joint actions to live them are healthier and more productive. Casper Mattresses actively demonstrated the power of their ideals during the pandemic by already knowing which alternate suppliers shared theirs. Even in the most difficult of times, they would not sacrifice integrity for sales. Transparency is of ever-increasing importance; technologies can simplify the process of providing it. No technology can force vision, mission, or core values. Those must be known and shared throughout the supply chain.

Employees

The concept of the lights-out factory was developed and promoted by makers of automation equipment. The goal? Eliminate employees and replace them with equipment. Wisely, that notion has washed into history for most manufacturers. No company has or ever will succeed and endure without employees, be they temporary, contract, leased, gig, or any other legal relationship. Without active, mutual respect, no manufacturing business can attract or retain the people it needs, regardless of the legal definition of the connection.

The work done by humans, both mental and physical, has changed drastically over the past few decades. Work content will evolve even more quickly in the next five to ten years. People are not interchangeable cogs in your money-making machine and cannot be selected or treated as such. Thinking skills, active passion for life-long learning, increasing comfort with ambiguity, willingness to take intelligent risks and learn from mistakes—these are the skill sets required to endure. No company can afford to exclude any group, whether from bias or ignorance.

Not only is the nature of work changing, but so, too, are the values of the employment base. Those who work sixty- and eighty-hour weeks routinely—and expect family to understand—are becoming rare. Work is not the meaning of life, though it is one means for each of us to improve the conditions of those we care about. We used to work long and hard to leave our children a better life; we've since discovered that our thinking was flawed.

If all an employee gets from working with you is a paycheck, your business cannot endure. Adults are making decisions about work based more on their own individual purposes than paychecks. When their values align with those of your organization, you both win. When someone leaves your organization for a nickel an hour, your business was not meeting their most basic needs.

Community at Large

The fifth—and often overlooked—constituency of every manufacturer is the community at large. This is not limited to a few surrounding blocks, nor even to the cities in which you operate. It has become increasingly obvious that the actions of some impact the many; that human beings living without clean water, food, or shelter is unacceptable, regardless of location; that abusive and unsafe working conditions are abhorrent; that what we do today impacts the future; and that the world comprises one people. Call all that human rights and sustainability, or simply consider that everyone matters equally. That is a constituency that no manufacturer can overlook. The poor, filthy children working fingers to the bone for eighteen-hour days are not lucky to have the work. They are unlucky that many consumers are blind to the impact of their purchase decisions.

Businesses may campaign against tax increases for libraries, schools, and better roads, yet they cannot exist without those things. In a desperate attempt to increase profits, some are unwilling to invest in what enables those gains. That is amazingly short sighted. During location decisions, organizations negotiate tax abatement and employment tax credits that a government offers to attract or keep them. While understandable, sometimes constituents need to be saved from themselves.

Several manufacturing companies have officially relocated headquarters to a low-tax country to minimize tax payments. Led by accountants, that is a financial move to benefit investors, with no offsetting benefit to other constituents. Yes, a different country might receive increased tax revenue, but the original one loses a great deal more. Minimizing tax payments is a strategy that serves no one well, including the manufacturer pursuing it.

Driving down the streets we can see that some companies let the building and grounds deteriorate, while others take pride in helping the community look and feel more attractive. We hear about businesses that give employees time to invest with the cause of their choice. Manufacturers can choose to support trade schools by providing equipment or teachers. There are a variety of inexpensive means to improving the community at large and benefiting greatly from that. Evidence shows that reducing water and energy usage and other sustainability practices pay for themselves. Being a good corporate citizen is not a loss leader.

Maximizing profits is not an effective intent. Using strategic profits to build an enduring manufacturing business is. Strategic profits require an understanding of mission, vision, and core values, and the importance of all five constituencies benefiting from the existence of the company. So, too, do determining appropriate agility, quality, and speed. Leaders who examine performance metrics of operators and suppliers and financial metrics of salespeople and customers may believe they have their fingers on the pulse. That is Delusional Excellence®. Endurance requires true excellence.

True excellence requires a purpose higher than profits, increasing benefit to all constituencies, and a passion for both. Without these foundations, efforts to improve are wasted trying to optimize a suboptimal business. Make your company matter consistently to many; then, over time, focus on ensuring the capabilities to deliver that on purpose continually.

VISION, MISSION, AND CORE VALUES: FINAL THOUGHTS

■ As transparency increases, consumers can make informed choices on something other than price. And they will.
■ Purpose does not have to be world-changing, and should not be quixotic. But if few share it, endurance will be elusive.

- Because every manufacturing business requires the help of its constituencies, focusing on value that matters to them as well as yourself is a requirement of building endurance.

Take a hard look at your mission, vision, and documented core values. Do behaviors and decisions reflect them consistently? Members of all five of your constituencies would love to believe in and care about the future of your manufacturing business. Make it easier for them.

Notes

1. *About Unilever*, December 2020, retrieved from https://www.unilever.com/about/who-we-are/about-Unilever/
2. *Truly Human Leadership*, December 2020, retrieved from https://trulyhumanleadership.com/?p=633
3. *Age Structure*, December 2020, retrieved from https://ourworldindata.org/age-structure
4. *Ratio between CEO and average worker pay in 2018, by country*, December 2020, retrieved from https://www.statista.com/statistics/424159/pay-gap-between-ceos-and-average-workers-in-world-by-country/;
   CEO compensation surged 14% in 2019 to $21.3 million, December 2020, retrieved from https://www.epi.org/publication/ceo-compensation-surged-14-in-2019-to-21-3-million-ceos-now-earn-320-times-as-much-as-a-typical-worker/;
   Why Do CEOs Make the Big Bucks?, December 2020, retrieved from https://www.salary.com/articles/why-do-ceos-make-the-big-bucks/
5. *About Us*, September 2020, retrieved from https://www.indsci.com/en/about-us/
6. (Cambridge Air Solutions), September 2020, retrieved from https://www.cambridgeair.com/

Chapter 3

Enterprise Capabilities

If you don't know which processes determine your future, stop until you do

The first two steps on the path to building successful and enduring manufacturing businesses are to grasp reality, and to commit to mission and vision consistent with core values. Those two will underlie the work, but alone are insufficient. A manufacturer must also effectively increase the provision of value that matters and do so profitably. Good intentions don't pay the bills.

Operational and Organizational Health

Your current capabilities will become insufficient, and likely irrelevant, sooner than you think. That is true regardless of industry. Financial success can delude us into believing we are better than we are. Despite standard statements on financial documents that insist past performance is no guarantee of future performance, many companies seem to believe it is.

Equally detrimental is a tendency to concentrate on protecting what we have rather than inventing new and better. Addicted gamblers aside, most traditional leaders hesitate to bet the house. Those who know what endurance takes are continually putting everything on the line for the mission and vision they pursue. It's not a real gamble, though, when passion for the mission, vision, and core values flows through the soul of the organization into strategic profits that facilitate the future.

Starting with Clayton Christiansen's *The Innovator's Dilemma*, we began to understand that when established businesses focus on protecting current products, they allow more aggressive companies with new technologies or solutions to disrupt them. Kodak is one famous example, but its lessons for us are often misunderstood. The company did develop digital cameras; they did invest heavily in them; they did create an online site for sharing. What the company failed to give up was its insistence that people print photos. It failed to adapt to a new business model for photography. Recognizing when to say yes and when to say no is exceptionally important.

Cannibalism is part of the analysis when considering adding new products to a portfolio. Perceived excessive cannibalism of a profitable product commonly interferes with future-looking decisions. Despite knowing the common lifecycle stages of a product, leaders often choose to extend and milk the decline period of existing offerings over the perceived risk of killing those products with new thinking. That was Kodak's big mistake. The best leaders know that products do not assure endurance.

That fear of taking a big leap may be logical to those who languish in ambiguity by keeping everything they can unchanged. Not every new product, technology, service, or business model is a good one, so occasionally being frozen by fear lucks into prudence. But fear in the face of ambiguity is not in the recipe for becoming an enduring manufacturing business.

A company that endures continually nourishes both operational and organizational health. In operations, it is easy to focus intently on improving production performance while overlooking our organizational robustness. We can't allow ourselves to fall into that trap. While there can be considerable overlap, the two aspects of the business have important distinctions.

Technology is the primary nexus in changing the mechanics of operations over time. Consider two-axis CNC to five-axis CNC to 3D printing as one example. No amount of manpower could duplicate those capabilities. Advances in computing led to the evolution of planning and scheduling from scraps of paper to Excel to MRP to ERP systems. But advancing technologies do not define operational strength.

Operational competencies that stand apart from the crowd demand a combination of well-designed processes and people continually learning, augmented by appropriate technology. Those are important. But so, too, are those organizational characteristics developed and sustained by a business operating system that frames "this is how we think and act." The second is what enables the first to continue over time. Mastery of both organizational and operational prominence is necessary.

Every business exists in uncertainty. Some thrive; most do not. Without the linchpins of mission, vision, and core values, an organization will be buffeted by external forces and internal vagaries. The more adept leadership becomes integrating organizational capabilities, the less ambiguity matters. The more agreement with the mission, vision, and core values, the easier it becomes to build requisite capabilities. The company is soundly tethered, but with a variety of alternatives in moving forward. Those lines eliminate most options, leaving a number of very good choices. With the right capabilities, making and executing a good choice becomes easier and the agility to modify on the run is also simplified. The key, then, is ensuring that the capabilities your organization focuses on are the ones that facilitate such movement and adjustment.

Most unknowns are noise, not signal, to your endurance. That may seem counterintuitive, but it is, in fact, what allows us to prevail. We can define and measure triggers on those external issues we suspect may become signal and not waste resources on the interesting but irrelevant. We invest resources on the opportunities most likely to move us forward. If a trigger indicates we should examine a force considered likely irrelevant earlier, we explore, learn, and make a decision.

What are the enterprise capabilities that enable good decisions coupled with the agility to adjust on the run? The first is a well-understood business operating system that builds "how we think and act" into everything you do. The second is limitless development of people. It is the responsibility of leadership to help employees reach their dreams. Their full potential in everything axiomatic to creating and delivering meaningful value in realizing the mission and vision is consistent with that of the business. The third is design capabilities extraordinaire: not only product design, but process design, operations design, strategy design, business operating system design, business model design, and constituency design (Figure 3.1).

Each of these three integral competencies, within its cost, quality, and speed characteristics, supports delivering targeted value to the mission. In enduring organizations, those essential attributes are never static, but instead reflect intensifying demands. Today's good is tomorrow's not-good-enough.

Organizations are commonly too wrapped up in today to invest time considering endurance. Thinking about the concept of a business operating system (BOS) is rarely prioritized on calendars. Designing it well gets even less attention. Development of people occurs in conversation, leading by example, and perhaps in a conference-room, one-to-many, expert-led workshop, but only if there is constant interest in the whole person. Training

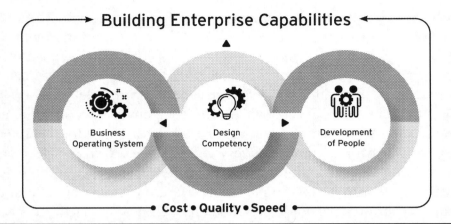

Figure 3.1   Building Enterprise Capabilities

is one of the first line items cut in any downturn in revenue or profits. Budget should not prevent fostering growth, and it won't if caring for every person's potential permeates the soul of the business. Yes, the form may change, but to reduce or eliminate helping people reach their potential is an all-too-common mistake.

Few manufacturing organizations can rightfully claim design as a true competency. High failure rates are common, yet often not recognized as such. Product design failures are almost expected along the way; eliminating them seems impossible. Hopes are common; robust expectations are rare. Minimum viable product (MVP) is an effort to ensure market fit, but it overlooks much of why design failures occur. Production processes are somewhat designed but are far from perfect in even the best environments. Additionally, many manufacturers would admit that most non-production processes they rely on are the result of evolution, not intentional design.

Leaders committed to building enduring businesses do not accept those conditions. The challenge in creating the competencies required is significant, but we have no choice. Shortfalls cannot be corrected quickly or at once, but we can address each with focus and expectations. The entire business will benefit when priority setting reflects the need for a robust BOS, development of people, and extraordinary business design capabilities.

Business Operating System (BOS)

A list of the common attributes of top manufacturers includes words such as agile, fast, resilient, responsive, leading, and trustworthy. Those capabilities do not require state-of-the-art equipment or technology; they reflect a business operating system instilled deeply throughout the organization. Modern equipment and technology can augment, but people and process are fundamental (Figure 3.2).

Certainly, if your business is in crisis, the top priority is to focus on immediate operational performance. For most leaders, the development of enterprise capabilities should take priority over the operations capabilities emphasized by daily productivity metrics. Those competencies may be more difficult to measure, but without them Delusional Excellence® is rampant. Giving due attention to operations is part of instilling the enterprise capabilities that will ensure the future of the business.

When I worked for Stouffer's during the 1980s, our president didn't sketch out a business operating system. He discussed the primary elements of that embryonic concept with every new salaried employee in small group breakfasts. He explained we would each be making hundreds of decisions daily—some small, some large. He would never try to be aware of, much less involved in, the vast majority of them. The decision-making guidelines he gave us were these: quality always first; the customer always second; cost always third. Our job was to assure the first while satisfying the demands of the next two.

As the person responsible for inventories and on-time, in-full delivery to customers, I sometimes requested the early release of a product that had

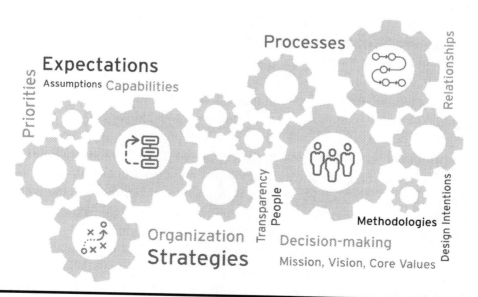

Figure 3.2   The Business Operating System: How We Think and Act

not yet completed all quality tests. The quality manager and I discussed the risks, impact on customers, and the costs of both sides of the ask. We both knew that he held the final decision. Our leadership team engaged in plenty of spirited discussions as we made decisions, but in the end, each of us understood why and how the final decision would be made.

In those days the company, owned by Nestlé, ingrained the elements of a business operating system, but not the systematized formality. Cultural expectations were sufficiently strong to ensure every employee could feel "how we think and act," if not put it into words. Your BOS does not have to be documented and can, in fact, be healthier if it is not. Documents sometimes approach religion, and religion is too often defended at all costs. An effective BOS should be living—developing further as you continue to learn and grow.

A dear friend had a go-to question when interviewing with a company for a leadership position. It was simply "what does it take to get paper clips here?" While that question would be framed differently today, it got to the core of the business operating system. Just how bureaucratic was the organization? How trusting and trustworthy? How flexible? How aware of important issues versus micromanaged detail? The answers to these questions have become integral to job and career decisions by younger workers. They want guidance, development, and a reasonable amount of freedom that is based on mutual trust. And they want to contribute directly to the success of the organization.

A BOS can ensure those reasonable expectations are met routinely. It defines relationships, assumptions, priorities, and, to some degree, methodology, while reflecting core values, mission, and vision.

People

In examining the organizational capabilities of an enduring manufacturing business, we find an operating system that promotes behaviors that enable people to thrive in ambiguity. All are confident in what they know and comfortable with what they don't. Agility requires nothing less. Trust makes that safe. We see processes that honestly assess the ramifications of decisions, both immediate and longer term. That disciplined openness supports agility and builds resilience. Employees recognize technology as an important enabler of people, knowing that the relationship of technology and people must be addressed continually, in line with mission, vision, and core values.

We find people who finish what they start, who are committed to Finish Strong®. Plan, do, check, act (PDCA) is a means of embedding improvement and lifelong learning, not an initialism with two meaningless letters at the end. The operating system defines clear and consistent expectations with organizational support to meet them.

The people I've just described exist in every company. Too many organizations waste them. Those employees become just a number in a turnover report issued by human resources. The critical distinction is not in the people; it is in how leadership prioritizes characteristics and recognizes that human beings are the gravitational force of enduring manufacturers. I talked with the owners/CEOs of two companies located within a few blocks of one another. One owner complained constantly about how difficult it is to find and keep decent employees. The other bragged about his wonderful team. Beauty is in the eye of the beholder.

An effective hiring process emphasizes demonstrated, passionate commitment to ongoing learning, coupled with insatiable curiosity. Hiring people for a specific skill that is likely to be unnecessary in a few short years may meet immediate needs, but it does not build your organization for the future. Nor does it develop the person who is the employee. Hiring those who are curious and able and committed to learning creates an agile workforce through a business system teeming with respect for human development.

It is highly unlikely that an organizationally capable business will be operationally incompetent. If it is, look for confusion in what operations should contribute. Pieces per hour is no measure of operations strength, nor is the amount of new technology. No company can expect preeminence through using equipment, materials, and science that is available to all.

Operational capability is not defined by product. It is defined by reliable provision of profitable value to the markets, consistent with mission, vision, and core values. Manufacturing operations can advance powerful competitive advantage in understanding and surpassing the needs of all constituents. Operational excellence is not a function of technology, but rather a result of solid process design that develops people while leveraging advancing science.

Design

In manufacturing, we know that design greatly influences customer acceptance, product cost, quality, and time to market. But looking at design as something that applies to little more than saleable products misses the point. From an industrial view, product design has evolved from basic, to design for manufacturability, to design for service, to design for reliability, until the current use of DFX as the all-encompassing initialism. Truly good product design reflects not only market considerations, but core values as well. For example, good design incorporates cradle-to-cradle sustainability in an organization that values the environment. Not cradle to grave; cradle to cradle.

Frank Lloyd Wright is considered a great design architect, but he wasn't. Most of the time, he wasn't even good. One of his driving design philosophies was form over function. That means when he believed he had to choose between the two, he always prioritized form. A building that is attractive but leaks and doesn't meet the needs of its owners or inhabitants is not a well-designed building. As art it might be fine, but as a product it is not. Consider him a good artist if you choose.

Good product design is rare enough, but embedded, great design thinking exists company-wide in only a handful of companies. Ozgene, an Australian-based biotech firm is one; Toyota of the 1970s and 1980s is another. Just over twenty years old, Ozgene is sufficiently new to have not faced a great number of challenges to maintaining its design focus over time. Its founder was open to the potential of business-wide design capabilities extraordinaire. The business operating system fortifies a complex adaptive system that, through integration of business microclimate-wide design considerations, is scalable, resilient, and robust. Their growth mechanism folds into existing thinking and design rather than trying to duplicate it.

Toyota eroded its embedded commitment to company-wide design mastery in the 1990s when it decided to expand production operations faster than its business operating system and extraordinary design capabilities could handle. They were unable to quickly duplicate much of what was critical; rather than slow physical growth they chose to lower expectations. Those expectations still exceed those of most manufacturers but returning ingrained thinking to a commitment to seeking perfection over very good is challenging. The company is currently working to recapture what made Toyota, Toyota.

Is your manufacturing business designed specifically to be profitable and enduring? Most begin with a product or a material and evolve into a business. One day we wake up to a company we know could be much better, but we aren't quite sure how to proceed. Every business evolves from that first product or material without emphasizing design for endurance. But the day you are no longer willing to live with what exists, you can begin the process.

Great design is embedded throughout the thinking of an enduring organization in everything it does. Shortcuts are not needed because speed, quality, and cost are intentionally part of every design. There are only temporary limitations, because if it is necessary, it will be developed. Great design is the breath of the organization, not a pocket of occasional creativity housed upstairs behind engineering.

Of course, great design businesses are subject to the same laws of physics, mathematics, and science that everyone else is; they simply push the edges of the concept of the possible. The theories of factory physics are leveraged rather than ignored. Disconnects are few and far between, because every important aspect of serving the purpose is considered in the design of the entire business system. Those designs are continually evolving as more is learned. Process bandages are not part of the thinking.

Processes are central to both success and endurance. They require design, measures of effectiveness, training, continuous improvement, and ownership by the people who work with them. Process execution requires discipline to build them into competitive advantage. Business processes, unlike those describing how production personnel make products, are often undefined at the execution level. Yet we wonder why variability and lack of robustness get in the way of effectiveness.

Production processes are often planned by engineers, sometimes with input from those who will be asked to work within them. But are those processes designed with targeted quality, cost, and speed characteristics defined? Are zero accidents or near misses considered? Are there product design decisions that should have been made differently? We are diligent in specifying exactly how workers should make product, but often less committed to designing a process that produces outstanding results every time.

Strategy, too, must be designed; that includes the strategy process and the strategies themselves. An executive offsite is not a strategy process; it is a work location. A well-designed strategic process is not an annual event. It is a means to create a living strategy that facilitates decisions within the bumpers, identifies when a review is needed, and then initiates that review. To be a strength of the business, that process must result in timely, appropriate guidance throughout the organization, reflecting all constituencies, to move along the defined path to mission and vision. The strategies it creates prioritize further development of competencies that provide a profitable competitive advantage.

The details of strategy development will vary by company. Strategic process design begins with the end in mind. What does a well-defined process provide as output, what inputs does it need, and how are those inputs utilized to create the output? We all need timely, relevant information, risk assessment, and a realistic evaluation of current and desired capabilities. Your company will have specific needs reflecting its current condition. In designing the strategic process, you will identify attributes of additional inputs and specify transformation processes to create the output you need. As your strategies and current realities evolve, so, too, may your strategic process. It should become faster and less expensive, while creating higher-quality output.

As our world continues to evolve, we cannot presume that our current business model is the most appropriate for us. The most common business model in manufacturing is along the lines of *buy stuff, change it in some way, and sell it*. Seems simple enough and hardly worth considering. But enduring businesses know better.

As strange as this may sound, leaders need to think deeply about what value is actually being provided to the market and what ownership, use, and financial characteristics best support maximizing that value. Manufacturers commonly add services to product sales. But *more* cannot be considered the default for how one company provides value to another. *Less* or simply *different* may be better for all involved. The design of your business model must reflect those deliberations.

While product-as-a-service (PaaS) is becoming more common, it certainly does not fit every manufacturing business. The key distinction is: Does your customer want and need to own the asset that is your product, or do they simply want what it can do for them? The business model that best meets the needs of your organization will also meet the needs of all your constituencies. Factory-as-a-service (FaaS) is developing from similar observations. Not every manufacturer needs to own every asset, and outsourced processing is not always the best answer. Capital-intensive businesses are becoming very interested in the potential of this model. It reflects the move toward a sharing economy and reduces the huge risk of many capital commitments.

Enterprise Capabilities

The purpose of enterprise capabilities is to fulfill the mission. Organizational and operational competencies, although with distinctions, involve mutual dependence and overlap. That is both intended and desirable. Endurance requires success, and success requires profitability. Profitability requires competitive advantage, which is a moving target. Competitive advantage requires true, not delusional, excellence. And true excellence requires prioritized strategic thinking throughout.

Enduring manufacturers know, and constantly consider, the enterprise capabilities to be built, improved, or retired. Questions such as "What changes could improve our agility or enhance its cost, quality, and speed characteristics?" are embedded in leadership thinking. Priorities change as knowledge, demographic, and socioeconomic realities do. As you take a hard look at your organization's capabilities, consider which aspects are most urgent and important to closing the gap between current and required conditions. Leaping that chasm is what positions your business to endure.

It is essential to fight the urge to look at your organization as an island, surrounded by raging seas. You have constituents interested in your success and endurance. Those relationships are integral to developing enterprise competencies. Looking outward for help while ignoring internal potential won't work; looking to your own resources at the exclusion of others is equally unproductive.

Healthy, mutually beneficial relationships are not easy, nor obvious. Endurance requires them.

ENTERPRISE CAPABILITIES: FINAL THOUGHTS

- The day you are no longer willing to be satisfied with what exists, you can begin the process of designing for endurance.
- Enterprise capabilities are not defined by your product. They are the thinking, integrating, and value-adding your organization has mastered that differentiate you.
- The more adept leadership becomes integrating organizational capabilities, the less ambiguity matters.

If your products and customers disappeared tomorrow, what important value could your manufacturing business offer the next day? If that's a difficult question, consider which processes and capabilities would enable you to replace those products and customers with even better ones in reaching your mission. Those are the enterprise capabilities to focus on first.

Chapter 4

Relationships Were
Easier in High School

All relationships require intentional work

No human is an island. No business is an island. And no future exists for either in a vacuum.

Thank goodness! None of us knows everything; none of us can be truly independent from others.

Businesses are social systems, technically enabled. That means that they consist of networks of people, institutions, and groups with a structure of roles and status. Those networks are relationships, be they distant and subservient, or tightly connected and peer based. Intention for those networks is integral to how they function. The use of technology in support of those systems is simply a means of distribution and connection, reducing the impact of distance and time.

Constituents, Relationships, and Strategy

Interacting with others can be an aberration, or part of a strategy. Strategically, we must have a definition of what a successful relationship entails. The question then becomes: Which relationships do we want to develop and maintain, or eliminate; today, tomorrow, and beyond? Relationship management is a common task within a sales team, but often it refers more to a software system than an orchestrated constituent-based strategy.

Manufacturing companies have multiple suppliers, employees, and customers. Most have multiple investor sources and numerous communities to consider. As key partners in success, those relationships, both as groups and individually, must be planned and executed by your entire organization. The initial success in those affiliations relies on if and when you choose to ally, with whom, and why. Even in transactional industries, relationships are integral to success. Healthy relationships do not require true partnerships; they do demand mutual respect.

While formal affiliations are not always worth the effort, mutually beneficial relationships are the only ones that work. If one party is focused on getting as much as possible, or giving as little as possible, it misses the point. Trying to take advantage of the other party lays down a flimsy transactional trail. Peer relationships, in which each party receives targeted benefit for equitable compensation, provide value to both parties. That is true among companies, people, institutions, and communities. Not all pairings are partnerships, and that makes sense. But if you are intending a path to endurance, consider all business interactions as occurring with individuals and organizations that matter.

Business strategy often looks internally and at customers and markets—no further. That limited view will not succeed. Identify all five constituencies and define the kinds of relationships your vision, mission, and core values implore you have with them. Then include needed work in the strategy and priorities of the organization. None of that can be an afterthought (Figure 4.1).

Not all markets are good markets; not all customers are good customers; not all orders are good orders. The ability to discern the difference is imperative. How do the various networks in your business social system know which are which for you at this time? Some manufacturers choose to focus on an industry (e.g., automotive), while others choose to avoid certain industries (e.g., automotive). Some avoid certain customers because of known behaviors, while others pursue only those who provide huge volume potential. Manufacturers occasionally specify a minimum order size to eliminate incurring more costs of satisfying the order than profits would cover. But do you want your salesforce to refuse a small order from an important customer because of that rule? I hope not.

You can walk through similar thinking for all categories of business relationships and quickly see how mission, vision, and core values play an important role in making smart choices. The business operating system must make clear these distinctions. While strategy has a shorter horizon, it will build upon that same thinking.

Example: Defining a Relationship With a Constituent

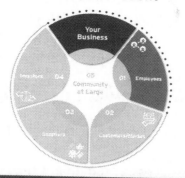

		1. Awareness **2.** Understanding **3.** Some Implementation **4.** Broadly Implemented **5.** Fully Implemented			

	Current Status	Current Strategy	Year-3 Target	Relationships with Employees	
				Permanent	**Temporary**
Mission	1	• Build into job descriptions • Start all meetings with this • Monthly supervisor/employee discussions of it and any concerns/misunderstandings	5	• Know, understand, care about, relate their role to accomplishing it • Help all partners internalize it	• Awareness on day 1 • How their work supports it every day
Vision	1	• Build into job descriptions • Start all meetings with this • Monthly supervisor/employee discussions of it and any concerns/misunderstandings • Relate our *what* to the vision during monthly town hall meetings	5	• Know, understand, care about, relate their role to accomplishing it • Help all partners internalize it • Understand how the *what* defines the vision	• Awareness on day 1 • How their work supports it every day
Core Values	3	• Emphasize safety at work, home, and in community • Monthly discussions of each core value, with witnessed examples and exceptions – develop employee response capabilities as needed • Address repeat offenders appropriately	5	• Know, follow, explain to others, correct others as needed • Ask questions, suggest enhancements	• Awareness on day 1 • Comply with corrections from others as needed • Bring exceptions they see to the attention of others
Enterprise Capabilities	1	• Identify what they are and how they can be observed in every job • Develop evaluation system for each major process and its current status • Identify best opportunities for meaningful improvement	4	• Comfort with the BOS • Know how role uses and impacts enterprise capabilities (ECs) • Enact/suggest changes to enhance ECs	

Figure 4.1   Defining Constituent Relationships

Do you try to pay employees as little as possible? The more an organization utilizes "find the lowest bid" processes, the less it cares about suppliers. Healthier partnerships work together to meet cost needs, while focusing on creating new value. While promised volume used as a carrot may seem appealing, does it really build the path you want to follow? Do you see the value in proactively communicating with investors, and they with you? Is your community proud to have you as a leader in advancing their interests? As you think through the kinds of relationships you want and with whom, consider these questions as positioning for the future, not meeting an urgent demand today.

Constituent Selection, Evaluation, and Development

Your leadership team needs to develop common understanding of how your purpose *can* and *should* impact each of your five constituencies. Those groups will impact your success in multiple forms as well. Intentionally build mutually beneficial relationships with each. That requires processes that are strategically aligned and well designed, measured, and improved as appropriate.

Manufacturers commonly have supplier selection and evaluation processes. When the former relies on price and the latter emphasizes delivery performance, enormous opportunity is overlooked. Both of those processes should be designed to reflect mutual strategic benefit, while reflecting core values. How do you make one another better and, combined, create progress toward both missions? That question should have specific, factual answers with each supplier.

Processes that define selection, evaluation, and development of each constituent group and the individual members will not boost endurance unless they specifically incorporate intended benefits to both parties. Together, executing audits of process performance against those targeted benefits provides valuable insights into strategic priorities.

Each business relationship should exchange core values, and each process review should incorporate consistency with those. A company that professes to care about people, but that works with a supplier that leverages child labor or has a high accident rate, is clearly missing something important. A business that declares commitment to the environment, but sources product from countries and businesses that allow harmful waste disposal, is misrepresenting itself. A manufacturer that declares partnerships, but has no focus on equity, is just tossing out popular buzzwords.

Whether considering speed and cost attributes, quality, or competencies reflected in agility, resilience, and responsiveness, all constituents impact your reality. If you are not intentionally identifying and maximizing their contribution to those, you are treading in quicksand. You have a responsibility to help them help you. That is one focus of constituent development.

We are all familiar with the concept of the weakest link. That point of limitation for your business may be internal or external, or at a connection point between the two. Not all change is equal because not all change, even when conceptually desirable, impacts results. The weakest link may dampen the impact of your efforts to improve.

An obvious example is improving the output of one machine when the next one is already operating at full capacity. The improved output of the first will simply create a pile of inventory in front of the second. There are better choices for where to focus attention.

Customers who extend payment terms unilaterally interfere with your progress. Relying on financial resources that cannot effectively support your anticipated needs limits your options. A community with poor schools impacts recruitment, employee development, your employees, and their families. Employees who don't trust you or one another cannot form effective teams, thereby limiting success.

Any of those can be a weak link, and one can be the weakest link.

While each group interacting with your business is important, they cannot all be the top strategic priority. As always, there can only be one top priority. It's difficult to make a wise decision without first understanding the potential impact of alternatives, both short- and long-term, based on present realities. Your process should include defined targets, accurate assessments of current conditions, and consideration of how best to close the gap(s) among or within the five constituencies. With that context, strategy can reflect the areas of focus positioned to help you take the most significant steps for organizational purpose. Lower priorities then can be identified and incorporated.

And as you consider what success looks like with each category, remember that each one is a collection of individuals and organizations and that none is a monolith. It is easy to view specific examples as representative of all or to focus on the concept of "on average." Your constituents do not look at your company's behavior that way, and endurance requires you recognize distinctions among and within groups. Beware generalizing from a specific.

If you don't care about and develop your employees, why would they care about your organization? True, they get a paycheck, but only the poorest are forced to work solely for that. Most of us would do any kind of work to provide our families with food, clothing, and shelter. Beyond that meager standard, other aspects of compensation rise in importance. Humans want and need to belong. Each of us wants to contribute. The vast majority of employees want to learn and grow. Do you know the hopes and dreams of each of your employees? If not, how can you know how best to create a mutually beneficial relationship? You'll be amazed by what your business receives in return when it provides those opportunities.

Jack Welch, former CEO of General Electric (GE), was known for his "forced whacking" of employees. Managers were instructed to force-rank employees and fire the bottom 10 percent. I can only imagine how much talent was wasted by biased managers. Individualized growth plans may have developed amazing new leaders. Teamwork no doubt reflected the television show *Survivor* more than the NASA control room that brought Apollo 13 safely back to earth. If someone is not a good fit, why wait for the annual cleansing to make a change? Who judged the judges? Even if those eliminated were, in fact, not deserving of employment with the company, how were they hired in the first place? Welch's edict was a reflection of a personal core value not likely posted on the wall, and company-wide processes that failed miserably.

When I first moved to Cleveland, Ohio, in 1978, I interviewed with three very different organizations. I accepted the lowest salary offer because the opportunity seemed to best fit my goals. I rejected an offer from an organization with a 20 percent higher salary primarily, but not only, because of their selection process. It was well known that they expected complete devotion from employees, meaning 24/7/365 availability. While not afraid of hard work and commitment, I heard the word "abusive" too often when asking others for insights into the company.

The CEO, not used to hearing "no" from a candidate, asked to meet with me to understand my decision. The company prioritized hiring graduates of Ivy League and other top-rated schools for leadership roles, and I did not fit that mold. They had insisted I take an IQ test. They then also required a psychological test. Finally, they made me a job offer with an outstanding compensation package and senior manager responsibilities.

My theory at the time was that if they couldn't tell that I am very intelligent without the IQ test, and they could not tell if I am a psychopath without the psych test, they were not very smart people themselves. I still firmly believe the first part of that, but I've come to understand that on occasion the use of psychology tools can improve hiring decisions. Some psychopaths are pretty good at hiding it. Most smart people can't conceal their intelligence.

The hiring process of most companies is less regimented than that, until senior roles are considered. A number of employee selection efforts are unofficially designed more to minimize perceived future legal liabilities than to identify candidates with the most potential to help the organization move forward. The further "down" the organization, the more willing manufacturers are to employ the "mirror test." That ridiculous phrase means if a candidate's breath shows on a mirror, hire them; it's the "warm body" requirement.

There is absolutely no excuse worth admitting for thinking about organizational needs that way. That approach reminds me of the driver sitting next to a blowup dummy while cruising the high-occupancy vehicle (HOV) lane. If the requirements to work within your company are that low, why should current employees believe you see them any differently? When managers finally remove a toxic employee, remaining workers usually sigh "it's about time." Employees are not stupid. If you treat them as such, you'll find mirror-test candidates are all you can attract.

I once fell in love with a résumé and made a very bad hiring decision. He had meaty degrees from top-notch schools, which I allowed to sway my evaluation of his potential. Within thirty short days, it was clear neither of us would be happy with his continued employment. He was polite, smart, and showed up reliably. Unfortunately, he had no interest in the role, the company, the industry, or learning from others. A capable hiring process would not have made the mistake I did. I realized the source of the error, but my employer had no real process to receive my confession and ensure others didn't make the same mistake.

When reviewing hiring and onboarding processes, time-to-contribute is a common, but poor, assessment concept. Do you know what you want a great employee to be saying or doing 90, 365, or 730 days after their initial orientation? Do you know what is important to them? Do they know what you are looking for? Are you thinking of a skill or task list, or contribution to an organizational capability? As with anything else, if you don't know where you're going, no road will get you there. When I joined Stouffer's it was crystal clear on day one that they had my best interest at heart, and that they fully understood my best interest was also theirs. All new employees should feel that valued, the first day and every day.

How manufacturing businesses think about ownership of assets and of people's time is beginning to change. The realization that people are core to the success of any operation is penetrating more deeply than ever. The legal and financial relationship with adults providing value-adding work to a manufacturer is often defaulted to "what we've always done." The formats of those relationships are really a strategic question. What evidence do you have that your current model is effectively meeting the needs of the individuals and the organization?

There are a number of employee models. In addition to the full-time employee tradition, contracting with employment agencies to provide temporary people, leasing employees, and direct contracts with individuals are common. Outsourcing short-term expertise needs to those with specialized abilities has become routine. The gig economy has grown significantly since 2015 and may not let up soon. With people integral to your success, it is important to understand the limitations and benefits of each of these models to choose wisely in each case. You may need to create a new one that better meets your purpose. Those kinds of intentional decisions can be optimized for mutual benefit.

As you review relationships with fellow employees—be they peers, contract, or any other type— consider your own biases, the current organizational culture, and what future you are working to create. Managers as a group may make generalizations about direct reports, and vice versa. Those thoughts reflect the degree of respect present. Additionally, there are one-to-one relationships within and among employee groups. All of these are important to the future of your company. While law requires you not discriminate, nothing precludes you from shaping relationships to best fit individual perspectives.

Just as manufacturers have employee selection, evaluation, and development processes, the same concept applies to each constituent group and the individual members of each. Individually and collectively, there are process speed, quality, and cost attributes, and impacts on target competencies that support agility, responsiveness, and more. There are stated mission, vision, and core values posted on the wall to guide each of these integral processes. It is important to design and execute constituent processes that fulfill all of those objectives.

Identifying optimal customer and market relationships is potentially complex, but like each constituent group, can be simplified. Customers who don't pay or pay late are plentiful. Big-name businesses that hold out the carrot of huge volumes can easily suck in the hopeful small-business owner and then leave them out to dry when times are tough. Not all will. The variety of markets served impact risk, cyclicality, and robustness of required systems. Choose wisely and it's great. Choose poorly and the future dims considerably. Strategic input is a necessity.

Some manufacturers sell goods and services to a transactional customer base, while others are relationship based. Often that distinction is based on the number and frequency of purchases as seen by the manufacturer. Some companies pursue a wide range of purchase frequencies to leverage both (e.g., selling both to consumers and to businesses). Those often require different capabilities, and perhaps even market strategies and organizational structures.

Transactions Benefit from Relationships Too

Don't believe for a minute that simple transactions should be absent relationships. Current technologies not only streamline transactions, but also enable personalized interaction. Bots are typically an internally focused cost-reduction effort, rather than a constituent-serving mechanism. As automation augments or replaces people, the enduring manufacturer will carefully design changes that enhance the nature of relationships.

Gas (petrol or electric vehicle charging) stations have widely transitioned from a relationship model to transaction-based, in which convenience and price drive sales. Unfortunately, that puts them squarely in the commodity space, where differentiation is less valued. Cleanliness and fill speed have become important factors, but both can be easily matched by any other station. Transactional businesses easily become commodity businesses and those tend to lower margins. When anyone else can copy everything you do, the odds of both success and endurance plummet. This should be obvious, but customer service and delivery mechanisms must consider the actual human customers.

Growing and processing poultry might not be your idea of manufacturing, but it provides important examples for each of us. When I was young, fresh chicken was as much a commodity as any product could be. Working for Frank Perdue and Perdue Farms in the late 1970s, I saw close up how a commodity could be turned into a brand and differentiated successfully. I saw vertical integration decisions, design and implementation of massive operational and logistics changes required to support new product and growth plans, and innovative thinking to reduce scrap to zero.

Perdue's leadership focused on helping his customers—grocery stores— sell more of his chicken with increasing margins. He knew that would build his business as well and open up more possibilities. Because of the promise of fresh, never-frozen product and the resultant short shelf life, his geographic market was limited. The company's brand building and operational changes supported his goals and those of his market, confined as it may be. Some challenges are best solved by seeing how to help others.

It is important to see how business strategy and operational capabilities are interwoven. The age-old question of which came first is, as with the chicken and the egg, unimportant. Identifying market, customer, and business needs may drive operations, or new potential operational capabilities can drive market, customer, and business strategies. Common vision and mutual respect enable both.

The first and most important determinant of good organizational decisions is defined mission and vision. Then, how does your product and service line move you toward those in a manner consistent with your core values? Perdue could have extended its markets one more state but chose not to unless and until they could operationally serve those geographies while maintaining quality.

The best organizations consider investors and the community at large—which includes the future—in a similar fashion to those discussed above. Every manufacturer has five constituent groups and cannot overlook any of them. Powerful examples are plentiful by simply observing the world around us. It can be crippling to take any group or individual relationship for granted.

Business Operating System and Constituent Relationships

I return you to the concept of the business operating system. That construct defines clear, mutually understood guidelines and priorities for interacting with all constituent groups. In some financially successful companies, those precepts shift with a change in leadership; in enduring companies the mission, vision, core values, and leadership principles remain largely unchanged. Strategies evolve, methods change, details are modified, but the fundamentals remain.

If you are not strengthening your customers, why should they continue to do business with you? If suppliers do not add to your capabilities, why would you buy from them? If your investors only supply funds when you don't need them, why would you be loyal? If you keep secrets from your investors, why should they risk their assets with you? If the community does not benefit from housing your company, why would it extend itself in your favor? If your business practices negatively impact the future, does the organization deserve to endure?

Business relationships, like personal relationships, can sour. If you were engaged in delusional partnerships, examine the reasons. Learn and build in any required changes to your relationship management processes. Sometimes people and companies are best served by reducing or eliminating interdependence as conditions change. That is neither good nor bad, just true.

The problem enters when a constituency is being failed and no one notices or takes action. Defined attributes of success being measured regularly, with predictive triggers in place, is not all that difficult. The COVID-19 pandemic brought to the forefront that relying on calendars to initiate supplier reviews is inadequate. Financial measures contain important lagging indicators, but impactful, leading success metrics are requisite to building your enduring manufacturing company. Just as we can't create a future we can't envision, we can't solve a problem we can't envision.

Hurricanes and tornadoes always lead to an outpouring of donations to the impacted areas. It's easy to see immediate need. With natural disasters, money is almost always better than goods, so it can be applied by local experts to meet the most immediate needs. During the pandemic, it was easy to see the hospitality industry suffer, so many ordered carry-out from favorite restaurants to help them survive.

Although not all needs are as obvious, recognizing and addressing them is important to managing important relationships. That takes vulnerability, transparency, interest, and current information. Highly visible needs change over time, just as the needs of your organization and its partners do. When sanitizing supplies were in short supply during the pandemic, I called a client and asked for a small quantity of his stock. He had converted some production capacity to making his own supply and gladly shared with me, just as he had with others of his constituents.

We cannot be successful or enduring if we take anyone or anything for granted. Just as in our home lives, relationships take attention, time, effort, prioritization, and a common concept of success. If you know with confidence that relationships with all constituent groups and parties are healthy and meeting the intended goals, your business can work through any obstacles it will face on its road to the future.

CONSTITUENT RELATIONSHIPS: FINAL THOUGHTS

■ Leadership requires a common understanding of how each of your five constituencies *can* and *should* impact your progress.
■ Peer relationships, in which each party receives targeted benefit for equitable compensation, facilitate endurance.
■ It is a problem when a constituency is being failed and no one notices or takes action.

Whether considering quality, speed and cost attributes, or competencies reflected in agility, resilience, and responsiveness, all constituents impact your reality. What one thing could you simplify to make it easier for them to help you?

Chapter 5

The Road to the Future

Hope is not a strategy, nor are financial targets

A world without Alzheimer's and all other dementia®.[1]

To accelerate the world's transition to sustainable energy.[2]

To organize the world's information and make it universally accessible and useful.[3]

benefit readers by acting as a free encyclopedia; a comprehensive written compendium that contains information on all branches of knowledge.[4]

enriching lives around the world with the safest and most responsible ways of moving people.[5]

The Role of Strategy

If any of these organizations waited to start until they knew the details of *how* to attain these missions, they would still be merely well-intentioned hope. You cannot create a future that you cannot envision. No one can afford to let the *how* part get in the way of the *why* and the *what*. We figure out *how* along the way.

That is the role of strategies. To figure out *how.*

As we learn more and as conditions change, the best approaches can take new direction. The destination remains the same. Strategies outline next steps and priorities along the path. Some of those steps remain unchanged for years, some for months. But the fundamental question remains the same: By executing our strategies, are we pursuing the most effective alternatives to make progress towards our mission and vision? (Figure 5.1)

Tesla provides an interesting example to consider. It may look like a car company, but it is really a sustainable energy company as its mission declares, making its *why* clear to all. Its *what* is a focus on battery development that efficiently maximizes renewable storage and minimizes drainage to power things, such as cars, that the world uses. The organization's development efforts are considering environmental impacts from cradle to cradle, sometimes more effectively than others. Tesla sells its famous cars, but also home solar storage devices, solar panels and roofs, roadside charging stations, and more. Each of those elements of the company's *what* requires a defined approach to become effective.

Because its elements of *what* are leading edge, Tesla knows the critical mass that each must reach to be financially and environmentally viable. The

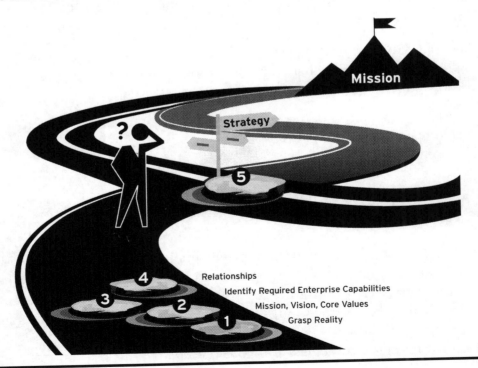

Figure 5.1 Which Is the Road to the Future?

individual plans are defined to get there, and then keep going. The company may someday sell off its car business, but it is unlikely to sell its battery business until they see a more effective *what*.

You have the *why* for your manufacturing company, or you know how to create it. You likely have the *what*—the avenue you pursue to best accomplish your *why*. For Ventana Medical—now a division of Roche—the *why* was "find cancer faster." The *what* was development of reagents and equipment. There were and are other potential approaches to finding cancer faster, but this is the one they determined, if only because of the scientific background of the founder, Dr. Tom Grogan, most likely to succeed. *How* then entered their picture. If the likelihood of success via that avenue becomes doubtful, the organization will shift its *what*.

The first four chapters of this book have described the initial steps that create the foundation for your path to endurance. You and your entire team have internalized that rapid, important change is a requirement for your business to endure, and more immediately, to succeed. You have personally and organizationally committed wholeheartedly to the mission, vision, and core values, recognizing their importance in steering your company through ambiguity.

You accept that product may reflect, but is not the basis of, competitive advantage. True advantage emanates from the thinking, integrating, building, and value-adding embedded in everything your organization does. Your organization knows that developing and prioritizing the capabilities integral to the future of your manufacturing business is essential.

Your relationships with all five constituencies—employees, suppliers, customers, investors, and the community at large—and the individual members within each, are indispensable in determining the best path forward. Those enhancements will be built into plans, priorities, and metrics.

Now it is time to identify the path you will lead your organization over as it marches, prepared, toward the future.

Strategy Development and Finalization

There are three primary elements of the total strategy process: development, finalization, and then deployment. The first two are discussed in this chapter; the third in Chapter 6.

First, it is important to have clarity on what strategy is and is not, and what output the design of your strategic processes should ensure.

Strategy defines the boundaries of the path your entire organization will follow in the near term to move ever closer to the vision and mission. In manufacturing, it has three major and coequal elements: commercialization, operations, and financial. Some think that commercialization is the only element, but it cannot be. It may not even take the lead. Tactics reflect strategy by defining the exact steps within the boundaries that will be taken and should not be confused with the strategy itself.

Financial goals are not strategy, despite conflation by many leaders. They are typically one of several metrics used to evaluate the quality of the strategy and its execution. Budgets also reflect strategies, but they are not the plan to move forward.

No single level, person, role, or function has all the knowledge required to define a complete and implementable blueprint. That is why endurance requires input from those who determine *how*, as well as those who continually assess the *what*. Reflecting insights of those elements provides the boundaries within which strategies will be defined.

As in production, the output reflects the capability of your strategy processes. A well-designed system provides a framework for differentiating development and finalization, and for effective deployment and execution, all fully integrated to enable each to be done exceptionally well. Its output provides guidance and incorporates requisite enterprise capabilities, appropriate relationships, and people. The content of that plan, which defines your road to the future, is the vehicle to create agility, responsiveness, and other capabilities you believe integral to success within the cost, speed, and quality parameters you specify in its design. It ensures that the intentions of commercialization, operations, and finance are aligned.

Strategy development and finalization are two distinct concepts, with finalization reflecting organizational agreement that the optimal path has been identified and responsibilities and accountabilities accepted. Many organizations consider development the same thing as finalization, a major thinking error that precludes endurance. The purpose of distinguishing the two is to reinforce the facts that neither top-level pronouncements nor executive offsite meetings result in a quality plan to move forward. Insightful feedback is indispensable.

As the fulcrums of the strategy are developed, it is important that they be examined by the people closest to them. Their wisdom is essential. Responding that they don't know how to accomplish the strategy is one thing; that it will have potentially undesirable secondary impacts another; and that the assumed elapsed time of major developments is inappropriate, yet another. Understanding implications may alter elements of the strategy. After it has been finalized is a poor time to recognize its shortfalls.

The process of bidirectional, multi-level, vertical feedback is called catch-ball in most lean manufacturing environments. The term is unimportant; the process is critical. It adds value in two distinct ways. One is that the feedback system contributes to an enriched strategy while building buy-in and understanding. The second is that the information needed to develop aligned, lower-level plans is in place.

There are many tools available to support strategy development. As with any methodology, it is necessary that your team understand when and why a specific contrivance is optimal for you. As an example, no organization can ignore the socioeconomic realities and expectations of its environment when defining strategy. Your process must capture relevant information and assess its potential impact. PESTLE is the acronym for one process intended to do that. It stands for political, economic, social, technological, legal, and environmental. Environmental scanning is another methodology. An internet search will uncover many more.

Those are best seen as checklists to reduce the odds of overlooking an important aspect of your surrounding world, and none holds real magic. Few tools are inherently good or bad; appropriate usage with an under-standing of the theory behind them makes all the difference. There is no need to reinvent the wheel, but it is always smart to understand what performance you truly expect and need from any wheel. For example, if a methodology does not incorporate assessment of your internal biases and preclude reinforcing them, it is likely not the best choice. Breathing your own exhaust can be deadly. Perhaps you can make adjustments that enable a tool to meet your needs, but only if you take the time to exam-ine it.

When the business strategy has been finalized, core assumptions and expectations of the lower-level strategies are defined. Those plans can be developed quickly, as the big questions have already been addressed. Finalization of those involves consideration of new details. As levels of detail intensify, inconsistencies that weren't apparent before become so. Competing priorities, typically in the form of resource availability, rise to the surface. Catchball of those elements, both horizontal and vertical, is again required. This is one of the many reasons why intentional knowledge sharing, both internally and externally, is crucial to the success of an enduring manufac-turer. Strategy is a living thing, and solid strategy relies on multiple sources of input.

As you identify your chosen path forward, you make assumptions. Those critical to the validity of your intentions must be clearly documented and monitored. Some will turn out wrong and a few of those will require that you make adjustments. Means to recognize and course correct when appropriate is paramount. A trigger system can sound an alarm when an erring expectation requires attention. Without defined critical assumptions and a trigger system, it is likely you will be caught unaware and unprepared for unforeseen challenges. Discussing the major "it goes without saying" beliefs also supports common understanding that will improve decision-making (Figure 5.2).

It is impossible, and not required, to consider all external and internal influences that could impact your business strategy. Shared commonality, seen through lateral connections, makes the various elements easier to assimilate. Those connections must, of course, be legitimate to be useful, but they simplify an otherwise overwhelming task. Perhaps an assumption about a developing Africa could be generalized into one about all second- and third-world countries, or perhaps not. It depends on the reason why that belief could impact your strategy. Consider important underlying premises in that light.

The concept of "a butterfly flapping its wings..." in chaos theory amplifies that everything is connected in a complex system. In the process of identifying your assumptions, do not get wrapped up in every single possibility you can imagine. Focus on risk, which reflects both probability and severity. Despite your efforts, something surprising will probably happen to impact

Key Assumption	Why it Matters	Trigger	Value to Trigger Review	Who owns Trigger
Market #1 grows at 10% annually for each of next 5 years	• We expect to retain share; growth depends on market growth	• Quarterly industry sales (per industry report) increase year-over-year	• Negative year-over-year growth in any quarter • Growth under 8% total in any consecutive 4 quarters	• Manager of business intelligence
Oil prices stay under $50/barrel	• High energy prices hurt our ability to gain new customers for Products A and B	• West Texas Intermediate Crude Oil prices	• Above $40 and rising 5 consecutive days • Stays above $45 for 5 consecutive days	• Purchasing manager

Figure 5.2 Assumptions and Trigger Systems

your plan. Prepare only for the most likely with medium to large potential impact. Paranoia is damaging.

You may feel that the strategy development and finalization process will take more elapsed time than the strategy itself will last. Not only is that not true, it cannot be true. As our worlds change more and more quickly, our strategies must be increasingly aware and responsive. As you develop and use these processes, solid design ensures agility is ingrained in them. Defining the current best path to the future cannot be an annual event; it must be a living process. Make the process increasingly robust, information flows in and out current, and mobilizing indicators visible. Doing so greatly simplifies both definition and execution.

Technology and Strategy

Today, technology threatens, empowers, and distracts most manufacturing industries and businesses. It needlessly confuses many strategies. Technology is not the goal; it is a potential enabler of improved paths to your desired end. The much-ballyhooed "digital transformation" is confusing that important distinction. That phrase, like operational excellence, is something many choose to claim because it sounds good.

With any technology, never skip asking *why* you would implement it within your company or with partners. Would your company be closer to everything it holds dear if it prioritized a digital transformation? Would your company be closer to everything it holds dear if it prioritized Industrial Internet of Things (IIoT)? Would your company be closer to everything it holds dear if it prioritized product-embedded sensors? Asking and answering these or similar technology questions, with specific answers, provides the guidance you need.

The abundance of developing technologies and applications can be overwhelming. Like the butterfly wing, it doesn't need to be. It is important, however, to be aware of the technologies most likely to add value to or disrupt your industry.

Develop a method to track classes of developing technologies, their primary use cases, secondary requirements, stability, and investment. Build a guiding thought process that prioritizes safety, scalability, and security into your business operating system. The relationships among information technology (IT), operations technology (OT), and product technology (PT) must be carefully designed. Confusion or inconsistent thinking has the potential to knock your organization off the tracks. Do not expect your internal resources to understand all this; technology is evolving entirely too fast, incorporating more and more aspects and integration challenges, for a traditionalist or hobbyist to stay sufficiently informed. Just as medicine has evolved into more specialties than we ever expected, computerization has as well. The devil is in the details; someone who can understand those details is not optional (Figure 5.3).

Regardless of how you choose to create and manage a system of staying abreast, that summary will enable a well-designed strategy process to educate and initiate technology discussions at a logical point. Prioritization, selection, and implementation should depend totally on how it supports your mission, vision, core values, important enterprise capabilities, strategy, and known challenges.

As an example, blockchain is a technology that can effectively provide provenance, traceability, and transparency. That technology also offers value

Technology	Primary Use Cases	Secondary Requirements	Stability of Technology	Safety, Scalability, Security, Speed
Blockchain	• Transparency/ provenance/ traceability is critical • Smart contracts	• Typically involves external partners, but doesn't have to • Pilots difficult	• Multiple backbones available • Stability good; make right choice on other factors	• Supports product safety • Reasonable scalability • Highly secure – that's the point • Speeds routine transactions
Augmented Reality	• Job simplification • Training • Safety	• Headware styles that work for various users • Loading/maintaining information	• High, and evolving • Hardware more at risk than software	• Promotes safety • Scalable • Requires data control • Speeds impacted processes
Machine Vision	• Inspection • Machine learning	• Provider hardware and software support	• Varies by use case, but stable in general	• Supports safety • Scalability is questionable • Requires data control • Impacts quality more than speed
Low/No Code	• Faster programming to meet business process user needs	• Carefully consider who can use it • Provider capability and support	• Concept stable • Consider when choosing provider	• Simplifies and speeds up programming • Other factors depend on specific application

Figure 5.3   Summary of Developing Technologies

in contract and asset management. If you and your market care about those, it would make sense to understand blockchain at a high level. Blockchain usually requires active agreement and involvement among multiple partners, which has implications far beyond the electronic. Your developing technologies summary, as input to your strategy development process, will highlight those factors and create important conversations.

Let your needs determine your technology choices. Manufacturers face a completely foreseeable exodus of aging, skilled workers, accompanied by challenges replacing those capabilities. Perhaps technology options, each with its own set of ramifications, should be considered to increase productivity, shorten learning cycles, or automate operations. As noted earlier in this chapter, intentional knowledge sharing is a must. VR, AR, and MR offer massive potential in addressing the challenge.

Technology often creates lingering costs and limitations, just as other major infrastructure investments in your business do. Estimating the "costs to undo" makes sense. The concepts of technical debt and technical capital have parallels in our physical worlds. They are akin to the limiting underbelly of traditional manufacturing investments and the empowering equipment we leverage daily. To understand technical debt, think of the locations of monuments in your operations that constrain flexibility. Then, like older equipment, add in the high potential that the technology will not be supported in the future. The "costs to fix"—ones that arise when shortcuts are taken to meet a deadline knowing full well that resources will be required later to overcome or fix those tactics—are also part of technical debt.

Whether it is old languages or old hardware and operating systems no longer supported, or underlying code that no one realizes is keeping your company operating, technical debt is a monster lurking in the corner. Designing in failure work is rarely the fastest, least-cost decision. The more technology we add, the more we potentially create. That doesn't imply that we should avoid technology; simply that a more thorough understanding of its future costs is worth gaining.

When leaders have invested so much thinking into these various integrated strategies, it is easy to forget that others do not have their level of understanding of the logic behind decisions. What is now intuitively obvious to the management team is in no way intuitively obvious to those tasked with detailed implementation. The best strategy, poorly communicated, understood, and executed, is little better than no strategy at all. Something this consequential has to be repeatedly discussed openly up, down, and across the organization to provide real value.

A well-designed strategy deployment process will close that gap, allowing the organization to realize the full benefits of its hard work.

THE PATH TO THE FUTURE: FINAL THOUGHTS

■ The fundamental question is: By executing our strategies, are we pursuing the most effective alternatives to make progress toward our mission and vision?
■ The content of that plan, which defines your road to the future, is the vehicle to create agility, responsiveness, and other capabilities you believe integral to success within the cost, speed, and quality parameters you specify in its design.
■ Defining the current best path to the future cannot be an annual event; it must be a living process.

Strong strategy requires both vertical and horizontal input in the decision-making process. Managing the right level of detail in the development and finalization processes is important to speed and effectiveness. Top–down strategy without that input is typically not implementable.

Notes

1. Alzheimer's Association, October 2020, Retrieved from https://www.alz.org/about
2. Tesla, October 2020, Retrieved from https://www.tesla.com/about
3. Google, October 2020, Retrieved from https://www.google.com/search/howsearchworks/mission/
4. Wikipedia, October 2020, Retrieved from https://en.wikipedia.org/wiki/Wikipedia:Purpose
5. Toyota Motor Corporation, October 2020, Retrieved from https://global.toyota/en/company/vision-and-philosophy/global-vision/

Chapter 6

The Fallacy of Trickle-Down Strategy

Gravity doesn't work for communications, nor does propulsion

Your defined strategy will be guiding hundreds of daily decisions throughout the organization, as well as setting significant priorities. If it doesn't, what is the point? But it can only provide that context if its implications are understood and integrated up, down, and sideways. Despite the hopes of many business executives, that will not happen by osmosis, nor edict, nor reliance on trickle down. It will happen only through a process designed both to ensure linkages, and that consistencies and inconsistencies are continually visible to all.

Business Operating System and Strategy Deployment

Over the first five chapters of this book, the concept of the business operating system (BOS) has begun to emerge. Every manufacturer has a BOS, whether well designed and lived, or comprising numerous fragments. Every company can benefit from the process of plucking those aspects of the business that are important, building processes to support them, and putting them together in a way that both internal and external participants know and feel.

Most manufacturers know they have a lot of smaller processes that typically occur within a functional department. Those processes, along with numerous, clearly identified categories of belief and behavior, begin to form the BOS. Too many believe the business to be functioning well, as long as product gets shipped and invoices get paid. That's like a doctor seeing a patient who can breathe and talk, and concluding they are healthy. Both completely ignore the system that ensures a healthy whole.

I remind you that a business is a social system, technically enabled. People are integral to its future. A healthy, well-designed system performs exceptionally well. A poorly designed or poorly understood system will choke and sputter, constraining performance potential. How humans interact within that social system defines potential and success.

The primary glue of a BOS is clarity and commitment to how the organization will think and act. While perhaps not obvious, this construct is the opposite of groupthink. It provides guiding consistency, not specific answers to questions. With meaningful mission, vision, and core values, the elements of the BOS begin to come together. Referring back to Figure 3.2, common additional components of a BOS include relationships, communication, decision-making and priority setting, critical organizational capabilities, and structures. Methodologies that reflect those considerations are often defined as well.

Strategy deployment is one of those ingrained methodologies that functions most effectively within the BOS framework. All too often, the strategy is defined at the top with expectations that it trickles down into the work content of every employee. If your company is one in which the strategy is not understood thoroughly by all employees and is not integrated into decision-making and priorities, your business is likely an example of the failed trickle-down approach.

Communicating Strategy

When I challenged the president of one of my first clients about the apparent lack of company strategy, he proudly opened his desk drawer to show me his strategy. It was written in French, his native language, but unknown by any other employee. It sat unshared, undiscussed, and irrelevant. I'm not sure how he expected to implement it.

Had he chosen to unveil his strategy to the organization, it might not have mattered. He had received no input. His lack of understanding about day-to-day business activities meant that he could not comprehend any prerequisite skill or process changes or any secondary impacts. His organization would not understand how what he revealed should intersect with current priorities.

That president chose to keep his strategy a secret. Top executive teams sometimes create a document shared only among themselves; others believe the budgeting process makes it clear. I've seen yet others hold all-hands meetings to announce the plan and then turn the troops loose to implement it, only to discover later that understanding and alignment were missing. That's one of the primary reasons the term "alignment" has become the buzz word du jour. It is commonly lacking, and with good, but totally preventable, cause.

Just as you designed a strategy development and finalization process, implementation requires a well-designed process as well. It will build lines of sight among all levels of the organization to strategic priorities, clarify connections, receive and incorporate feedback, and define meaningful metrics that highlight both progress and exceptions. Because your strategy considers all five constituencies, parts of it will be executed with external partners. Deploying the strategy with them must be part of process design. The outcome is that each participant is positioned to do the job well in a way that propels the organization forward along its chosen strategic path.

Executives can rightly choose to keep parts of the strategy close to the vest. Those are typically shifts in direction that they don't want competitors to know in advance. Yet some partners must be involved in defining and executing those priorities. A well-designed process will allow for this.

Verifying Strategy Implementation Decisions

Effective implementation requires a tight, two-way methodology as strategy flows into execution, and challenges and opportunities uncovered in that process flow back to strategy. The path your business intends to follow may need to have a few stones moved slightly or replaced with ones better fit for your intentions.

Most of you are familiar with a problem-solving tool called The Five Whys. You may not have used it personally for years, but it has value beyond daily shop floor challenges. By utilizing five-why thinking, the team can identify the root cause of the problem experienced. The real value of the tool comes with working back up the chain using "so that." If it makes sense that direction, you likely have identified the true root cause (Figure 6.1).

This same type of two-way thinking can tightly connect the strategy you intend, and the tactics identified to execute it. It ensures that every constituent understands how they contribute to organizational success.

This thinking can—and should—also be applied horizontally. While it may seem that a manager will ensure horizontal consistency among their direct reports, as we move up the traditional organizational chart, that becomes increasingly difficult for a single individual to do.

Referring to Figure 6.2, consider that this vertical, bidirectional testing is happening across the entire organization. The example strategy of reducing build/ship lead time to less than two days requires more than the tactics listed. Some of the additional work likely must be identified and executed by people not working for Manager #1. Perhaps the cooperation of purchasing, which reports through the same executive, will be integral to success. How would purchasing know that, and how would we ensure this plan is consistent with their other priorities?

After you've challenged vertical alignment, it is important to identify horizontal resources and cooperation that will be important. This will typically include both internal and external expertise. Once again, the concept of key assumptions comes into play. These details should not be considered showstoppers in the strategy development and finalization processes, but they can require rethinking how the high-level strategic elements will be accomplished. The interactive process of multidirectional testing will occur throughout deployment. Your strategy will be lost in those activities if you

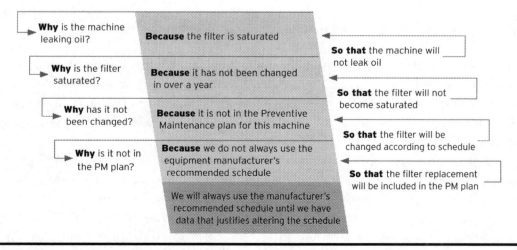

Figure 6.1 Problem Solving: Example of Bi-Directional 5-Why Thinking

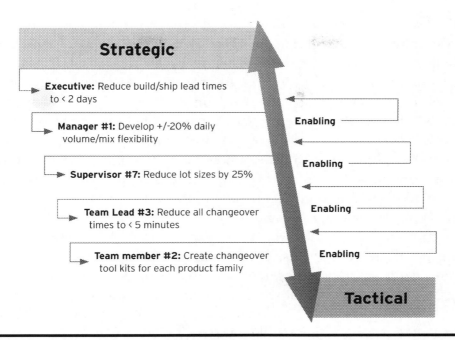

Figure 6.2   Strategy Deployment: Example of Line-of-Sight, Bi-Directional Thinking

do not actively maintain the line-of-sight visibility of tactics to higher-level strategies. Alignment is not one-and-done.

Consider the current system you use to share the finalized strategy with all those involved in executing it. Do you have an effective methodology for both vertical and horizontal feedback, prioritization, and visibility? Is your strategy alive? None of us has a perfect process, but we can each improve how we move forward by evaluating these questions.

A business operating system (BOS) can build in this kind of verification thinking as routine in all decision-making. The applications beyond strategy deployment are many. This example can be part of the way your organization thinks and acts about decision-making, about communication, about priorities and more, but only if you build it in. Without something similar, lazy assumptions become too easy. "Because it sounds good" should not drive action.

As you bring aspects of your ideal behaviors and thinking out of the fog into elements of the culture you are building, the BOS for your company takes shape. It can provide consistent guidance, priority calibration, and keep the business focused, if you live it. All constituencies believe what they experience, not what they are told. A commitment to respecting and developing people and the promise of mutually beneficial relationships are hollow without persistent follow through. Leading a company is not easy. Consistently living every element of the BOS is not optional for an enduring manufacturing business. Neither is improving it.

Documenting critical factors within the BOS can enable conversations that are important, perhaps now lying under the surface until they are specifically acknowledged. Keeping them documented can imply and increase resistance to change. So much of effective leadership is recognizing and walking fine lines that can make a huge difference in your ability to build an enduring organization. Few one-time mistakes are fatal; simply learn what works best for you currently and be open to changing when something isn't contributing to progress.

A litmus test can be valuable as you analyze and define your BOS. Your test is not likely the same as someone else's, as your company is its own organism. Observing the best in other organizations that you want to emulate, as well as observing other factors that you do not want to be part of your business, provides a good framework. Usually a handful of factors is sufficient to test for validity and consistency (Figure 6.3).

All the processes described thus far create conditions to make it easy for each person to successfully execute responsibilities and accountabilities. They are in no way micromanaging, but instead, are providing freedom within understood borders. It is the role of strategy deployment, or implementation, to keep those boundaries clear as reality rears its ugly head. Or its exciting, energizing head. Or its distracting head. Or its confusing head. A well-designed strategy implementation process ensures attention on the things that matter most.

The Power of *Why, What,* and *How* Together

One of the most common *how* challenges is keeping the *why* and *what* uppermost at all times. It is entirely too easy to get wrapped up in details of doing. Most factories I see with floor-level metrics focus on Safety, Quality, Delivery, and Cost. Some add an E to the end of that for Engagement. I would hope that the strategy of a manufacturing business that wants to be successful and endure over time would demand much more out of operations than simply the basics. Those four or five letters (SQDC-E) should be improving simply because of core values. Yes, each one can point to a section of strategy, but enduring manufacturers consider those table stakes.

ABC Manufacturing Company

Does it…?	Absent 1	2	3	4	Complete 5
Define our identity well			●		
Make it easy to do the right thing in the right way		●			
Provide guidance to all important actions and decisions				●	
Build energy within all aspects of our business	●				
Provide the basis of innovative thinking			●		
Enable improvement		●			
Facilitate breakthrough thinking	●				
Reflect our mission and vision and lead us there					●
Support strategic profits rather than maximizing profits				●	
Facilitate extraordinary design throughout the business			●		
Recognize when average is good enough and when it is not				●	
Leverage design competencies	●				
Integrate development of all people					●

Figure 6.3   Business Operating System Litmus Test Example

Many of us are familiar with the story of Alcoa under the leadership of Paul O'Neill. He took the helm of the aluminum maker and oversaw a more than 80 percent reduction in the rate of lost workdays caused by work-related injuries in his first year. He cared deeply about people. Upon his arrival at Alcoa, Mr. O'Neill found the injury rate atrocious. He knew that if he personally emphasized safety, everything else would improve markedly as well. And indeed, it did. Quality, delivery, costs, and engagement all improved as a result of his devoted attention to workplace safety.

Those successes were a function of how he created responsibility and accountability for workplace injuries up, down, and across the entire organizational structure. It was no longer simply a floor-level concern. In the process, a new culture was established, and a new business operating system evolved. Then the organization was ready to define and implement additional strategies to move the business forward.

Had Mr. O'Neill's insistence on knowing the facts of every workplace injury in a short time frame waivered, the attention of the entire organization would have as well. A powerful leader who continually demonstrates *why*, *what*, and models the core values creates the space for others to accomplish the seemingly impossible. Those who worked at Alcoa would not have believed the operational numbers could have been so positively impacted in such a short time had they not experienced it.

Alcoa is not an example of trickle-down strategy; it is an example of voracious attention to critical variables embedded in the organization. Paul O'Neill did not simply tell his top staff to improve safety and trust that it would happen. He did not rely on monthly or quarterly reports. He built safety into every leadership conversation, which then required that those leaders build it into each of theirs. They could not have met his demands any other way. Notice also that he didn't stomp his feet and shake his fists and then move on to other challenges. Nor did he tell his team how to assure the safety of employees and visitors. Living what is important and urgent brings clarity for others, as they identify and execute what they see as best in meeting those expectations.

For strategy to become embedded in the decision-making and actions of your organization, you—the leader—must keep it front and center across your leadership team. The commercial, operations, and financial parts of the organization must never lose sight on *why*, *what* or the path you are now walking. While strategies have many elements, there can only be one top priority to an organization. Agreement on that precludes wasted time. Alcoa under O'Neill demonstrates that as well as any example could.

Your company may not have a single point of pressure, like Alcoa's safety, that can singly thrust it forward. But it may. It could be slow decision-making, unwanted employee turnover, or something else that interferes with progress. Your strategy process should consider that question with in-depth thinking, identifying that lever if it exists.

One common challenge in strategy deployment is letting go of decision-making. As leaders, we often believe that we know the best way; that we see and know things that others do not. An executive who insisted that his team make most all decisions told me that one of two good things will happen. Either he'll learn some things that he didn't know, or the team member will learn things they didn't know. In most cases, he insisted, it's a bit of both.

As you design your strategy deployment process, don't forget to build in specific learning steps. The methodology of after-action reports (AAR) isn't limited to military exercises. It is, in many ways, another version of PDCA in action. If you want to build a learning organization—and the intention of an enduring business requires that you do—infuse that into your business operating system and the processes within it. Weave it into your internal and external relationships. Make the joy of learning, even if that learning is a painful lesson, part of daily living. Only then can implementation of strategy accomplish all that it offers.

As we develop and deploy our intended plans, it becomes important that strategic thinking is not a skill limited to the corner offices. Many departments in manufacturing businesses, especially in operations, have been taught to think and act tactically. To build an agile and responsive organization, conceptual thinking capabilities must spread throughout. The "get order, fill order" mentality does not fertilize the seeds of an enduring manufacturer.

THE FALLACY OF TRICKLE-DOWN STRATEGY: FINAL THOUGHTS

- Your defined strategy will be guiding hundreds of daily decisions throughout the organization, as well as setting significant priorities. If it doesn't, what is the point?
- Strategy implementation will build lines of sight among all levels of the organization to strategic priorities, clarify connections, receive and incorporate feedback, and define meaningful metrics that highlight both progress and exceptions.
- Alignment is not one-and-done.

Verification of significant decisions and actions by overtly connecting them to the strategy should be built into leadership discussions. Similarly, all employees should be able to connect their priorities and decisions to the strategy. That is how line of sight provides alignment throughout the organization.

Chapter 7

Transitioning Operations from Tactical to Strategic Thinking

"Get order, fill order" is no way to run operations

This book is written for executives of manufacturing businesses. The principles espoused, however, can benefit a wide variety of industries, whether service, medical, retail, or high tech. Those organizations all have operations too, but this is one area where manufacturers have a somewhat unique set of challenges.

Operations personnel in manufacturing have traditionally been rewarded for tactical thinking and pulling rabbits out of hats. That head-down, hero mentality is expensive and ineffective in creating and delivering value. Unfortunately, it is built into the thinking of many employees who like being heroes and many others who like having heroes. Fundamental changes in thinking processes are required throughout the manufacturing organization. Transitioning operations from reactionary, tactical behaviors to strategic focus on defining and delivering increasing value is especially urgent.

Escape the Cost-Center Mentality

Cost accounting. Financials. Cash flow. Bank covenants. Depreciation. Write-offs.

Seen as the group responsible for costs in manufacturing companies, operations is often judged by financial data. Joining the ranks of management requires an increasingly thorough understanding of each financial and accounting topic.

Most manufacturers use some form of standard costing along with all its variances. Accounting and leadership expect those in operations to explain those variances monthly. It's difficult enough to remember what happened yesterday, much less weeks ago. The details that created variances are rarely top of mind.

Because operations is typically considered a cost center, its leadership must attempt to manage costs the way the organization reports them. This constant attention to historical standard, reported operations costs, and the resultant variances leads operations management to look backward at often-misleading details rather than forward at the big picture.

I realize many executives believe all the work put into creating standards for material, labor, and overhead—reporting against them and then trying to explain variances—brings great value to the organization. If they didn't believe that, they would likely find a way to stop spending the time and money it takes. I encourage considering higher-quality alternatives that better support timely decision-making. For now, I'll let go of most of that. I simply ask that you consider not using monthly variances to drive any decision-making of consequence and that you don't waste valuable time researching and explaining them. Instead, insist on receiving information where and when you need it in order to help your entire team make better decisions. Time is better spent figuring out what those insights are and how to reliably gain them.

I am not at all suggesting that operations ignore costs. I am simply saying that the standard cost accounting monthly ritual is not an effective means of understanding and managing costs, and more importantly, that the potential contribution of manufacturing to business success is dreadfully limited by the cost-center mentality.

Most budgeting processes in manufacturing organizations insist on cost reductions from operations. Supplier and logistics price reductions from the supply chain, and labor cost and scrap reductions from production, are often expected. Parts and product rationalization and, in most cases, superior design, can have a much greater impact. It might not be seen in most standard costing systems, but it will be found in profits and cash.

Understanding total cost of ownership (TCO) and better yet, supply chain total costs (SCTC), would be far more effective in moving your organization toward the mission and vision about which you care deeply. Insisting purchasing negotiate lower prices with suppliers may seem obvious, but it is often a damaging expectation. The bad thing about incentives is that they can create poor decisions. Shifting costs of any kind from one supply chain member to another belies mutual benefit. It makes more sense to work with suppliers to reduce TCO and SCTC. Reducing time and variability can have a much greater positive impact than price reductions.

No business can cut its way to success. Cutting costs has a bottom limit. Yes, that "unfavorable labor cost variances" line on the expense part of the profit and loss statement looks like an easy target, but it does not hold the key. Cheap labor is not the Holy Grail of manufacturing, even for self-identified commodity businesses. Looking at operations as a cost center instead of as a value creator is extremely short sighted.

To thrive in the twenty-first century, both the commercial and financial elements of the business must think about operations differently so that operations themselves can do the same. The concept of "cost center" puts a negative connotation on what should be a major strategic contributor to providing increasing value to all constituencies.

As the organization begins this shift in thinking and behavior, operations personnel can transition as well. The result can be proactively designed capabilities that the world awaits. Operations leaders may have lost those vital skills through the constant reinforcement of tactical priorities. They can be regained and grown when that matters more than explaining variances. It is all about clarity on what is most important. How time is spent and human development is prioritized demonstrates that guidance more than does any pronouncement of changing expectations. Cultivating strategic thinking skills throughout the organization should be ingrained in the business operating system.

As your organization shifts from the "get order, fill order" cost mentality to a strategic, value-adding business operating system (BOS), it is time to build and leverage your operational capabilities.

Demand Responsibility and Accountability for Customer Satisfaction and Retention

As described in Chapter 5, the three co-equal elements of a manufacturing business are commercialization, operations, and financial. Common departments (e.g., product development, engineering, IT, sales, marketing, treasury) serve those purposes. The business operating system, extraordinary design capabilities, and development of people that underlie development of enterprise capabilities in your transition to endurance can ensure each element is aligned and working together with the others. Responsibility and accountability may shift during those processes, but they must always be clear and accepted.

Consider commercialization as developing and managing markets, customers, and distribution channels; gathering market intelligence; identifying market price levels for various value propositions; and perceiving unmet market needs. Finance provides oversight and insights into all revenue and cost factors, treasury functions, non-product and non-service compliance, and overall risk management.

Operations' accountabilities and responsibilities include proactive product and service development, supply chain relationships, reliable delivery of promised value to all customers, customer service, satisfaction, retention, and more.

Most manufacturers are organized as if the commercial function is responsible for customer satisfaction and retention. But it is the performance of operations that determines those. Perhaps commercial personnel in your company have not trusted operations to satisfy and retain customers. Based on compensation structures, sales personnel often work to keep those relationships to themselves. But to whom does sales go for answers? Operations.

Figure 4.1 provided an example of how to define targeted relationship characteristics with each constituency. Refer to those that your company developed for your markets. There is no reason why a customer's sales contact should change, but operations should have accountability and responsibility for customer service, customer satisfaction, and customer retention. This thought process has the added bonus of integrating customer relationships with the organization and not with a specific salesperson.

By demanding accountability and responsibility for customer satisfaction and retention, leaders in operations must think more strategically. Their role is no longer ensuring capabilities and capacity to "get order, fill order." It becomes knowing and anticipating market needs and wants and determining the supply mechanisms that best develop value performance for the organization. It requires expert involvement in both strategy development and execution as well as the business operating system, while mastering forward-looking design. This isn't your father's manufacturing environment.

Strategy without execution is just a dream, but execution outside an umbrella of strategy is myopic and doomed to fail. Two perhaps not-so-obvious truths: manufacturing is a supply chain decision; so too, then, is the choice of vertical and horizontal integration.

Those decisions can go very wrong if not planned and executed well by operational experts. Look to the Boeing 787 Dreamliner. Or the "Nightmareliner" as many began calling it. Boeing chose to transition from a vertically integrated manufacturing model to a global-partner model in the development, design, and production of a product deemed important to that company's future. Numerous quality problems arose from both commercialization-driven priorities, and design and machining weaknesses in many components. Poor communication and inconsistent assumptions were rampant. There's a lot more to outsourcing than issuing contracts and purchase orders. Boeing executives became acutely aware of the volumes of tribal knowledge and "off-the-record adjustments" that had previously kept production moving.

With the shared insights of commercialization and finance, operations can proactively develop profitable products that the market will buy, ensure reliable delivery of value promised, and serve and retain customers. By becoming engulfed in furthering enterprise capabilities, it can propose potential capabilities to commercialization and finance. Not simply new machines. New capabilities that could create amazing value. Consider how Rolls Royce uses data from its jet engines to advise customers on fuel efficiency, improved maintenance, and better flight plans.

An enduring manufacturer is always searching for better ways to create and deliver more value in support of the mission. Operations, if focused on tactics and separated from both customers and the market, cannot contribute to that crucial priority. Commercialization and finance cannot be successful without them.

Close the Chasm between Strategic and Tactical Thinking

We all know the expectation "faster, better, cheaper." That alone will not position your business to last another twenty years, much less one hundred. Offering new colors or bundled packages or faster product performance won't enhance endurance. Five years from now, do you believe your customers will accept the same solutions your product and service currently provide?

If your customers' value-adding thinking isn't evolving quickly, you're in a dangerous market. If yours isn't either, you're in a dangerous business.

How do you transition operations from a tactical, firefighting mindset to a big picture modus operandi focusing on what the future should be and how to best create it? The first step is always an accurate grasp of current conditions—in this case, how strategically your organization and operations team currently think.

One of my consumer goods clients discovered that they weren't really managing inventory, much less thinking strategically about it. That lesson was borne in an email from the CFO asking why inventories had risen by $2 million over the past few months. The company was growing, and everyone was busy. The focus was on keeping production and shipping going, not on inventory investment.

A senior planner was given the task of analyzing inventory and developing a plan to keep it under control. For both raw materials and finished goods, he created a data export of month-end inventories in units and dollars and wrote a formula to calculate weeks-supply based on current demand projections.

He looked first at parts and materials with what he perceived to be ridiculously long weeks of supply. He issued memos to sales and purchasing, noting those identified problem children and asking those groups to take action to reduce those inventories. He then reviewed the various product categories, averaged the weeks-supply of each, and issued a memo telling both planning and purchasing that these were the new maximum inventory levels by category.

His next spreadsheet calculated the projected dollar value of inventory when his "strategy" was implemented, and he shared it with the CFO and the VP of Operations. Without pursuing the underlying thinking, they said the numbers looked good and moved on to what they believed to be their next highest priority.

Let's examine a few problems in this scenario.

First, why were problematic inventory dollars identified by the CFO instead of by operations, and what was the "right" investment level for their inventories in that period of growth? "Higher" could be more or less appropriate than the prior level. That 30,000-foot-level, total-inventory-dollars number is practically useless on its own. We've all experienced excess inventory of one item while facing shortages of others. Operations should always provide forward-looking dollar inventory projections to finance, coupled with an explanation of why.

Next, the planner's process was mechanical, and no doubt to him, logical. But there was, in fact, no strategic thinking in that methodology, nor was there analysis of implementation requirements. The executives simply wanted the problem handled; they didn't insist on or verify that his work provided an ongoing strategy to optimize inventories to deliver brand prom-ise. They and the planner both considered an inventory plan in place when there was no such thing.

This organization did not think strategically.

They believed every operational decision other than how much to make today or how to put a bandage on a production problem to be a strategic one. Buy equipment to replace that injury-prone human activity? They con-sidered that a strategic question. And it could have been. But was there any overall commitment to creating an environment free of near misses and accidents? Was there any prioritization? No. They had several minor injuries from that step in the process, decided one day to explore automating it, and then bought a machine to do so. The decision was a reaction. Nothing more, nothing less.

So, what differentiates strategic thinking from tactical thinking?

There are an infinite number of paths from Point A (current) to Point B (vision/mission). As discussed in Chapter 5, the business strategy provides the framework of the path that the organization will take. It provides the touchstone for important decision-making. In support of that are the com-mercialization, financial, and operational strategies. The latter becomes the touchstone for major decisions such as infrastructure, supply chain, and technology.

In the case of our inventory problem, the tactical approach used no standard to guide it. "Reduce inventory" is an order, not a strategy. As such, it does not tie to the overall business strategy, lower-level strategies, relation-ship or capabilities intentions, mission, vision, or core values.

How did the "solution" integrate supply chain conditions or customer needs and opportunities? It didn't. How did it ensure implementation and success? It didn't. It was a tactical response to a tactical order: a reaction to a perceived problem that was neither well understood nor defined.

Similarly, in the case of our unsafe operation, the decision to automate was not tied to any strategy, mission, or vision. It might have reflected a core value (e.g., provide a safe work environment), and in fact been a good deci-sion from that perspective, but it again may well have been a short-sighted solution to a problem not well understood or defined. Was the operation needed at all? How did it fit in the overall process? What options were con-sidered and rejected, and why? Extraordinary design capabilities would build in this thinking.

To embed strategic thinking throughout operations, leaders must con-stantly remind decision-makers, which is everyone, of the criteria provided by the strategy. Questioning how options considered are consistent with those standards should be routine. The bidirectional verification thinking described in Figures 6.1 and 6.2 can be a common communication tool. Personnel will learn to answer those questions before making a final recommendation or decision. They will learn to check horizontally as well, as others may be involved or impacted. Considering all constituents becomes standard procedure. That is when the troublesome chasm between tactical doing and strategic comprehension is closed.

Design Structural Aspects to Facilitate Speed, Agility, Flexibility, and Robustness

Not every decision is strategic, but every decision should be guided by strategy. The much-discussed concept of alignment requires that. The components of strategy address the primary questions integral to effective progress. Many of those are structural issues—decisions that are more difficult, time-consuming, and expensive to change. As the speed of commerce continues to accelerate, reducing the length of commitment to these structural investments becomes ascendant.

The move of operations from developed to low-wage-rate countries was largely driven by accounting, product management, and the search for lower costs. The manufacturers who chased low labor costs might argue they were strategic, but most were not. They were reacting to price pressures and saw cheap labor as the answer. By focusing only on that one aspect of cost, they overlooked the impact on every other part of the business—especially the missed opportunities to make significant improvements within their own company and supply chain. The impact on skilled labor availability was only recognized and became a concern during the post-2009 economic recovery as companies looked to re-shore or grow domestic production and couldn't find the people they wanted. The time, difficulty, and costs of undoing the ramifications of that set of offshoring decisions are significant.

Was there an overall strategy to produce in the geography where customers existed? As global business spread, that approach seemed reasonable, but it also added levels of complexity insufficiently considered. Those who developed global operations strategies without adequate consideration for international geopolitical risk, the predictable rise in wages in growing economies, or the impact on domestic skilled labor may have simply defined a bad strategy. Being wrong on important predictions is one thing; not thinking about those very predictable eventualities is another. Do you have the competencies to expand your business operating system globally? Not everyone does.

Looking back at Ozgene, the company has added operations within the design parameters of their business. Consider the approach more "plug and play" over "copy/paste." They expand slowly to ensure the organization knows how to maintain the focus that matters to their endurance. They don't assume success; they design it in and execute a version of PDCA to ensure success. In early spring of 2020, that company was able to stand up COVID-19 testing in the Caymans within one month. They worked with the government, the hospital, and their own systems and processes to make that happen. Because Ozgene has capable processes for building strategic partnerships, interactions with those new, external resources could be integrated with new lab processes quickly and effectively.

An effective business operating system includes a process for staying abreast of evolution and revolution in the markets, the supply chain, technology, and socioeconomic and political realities. The development of the Internet of Things (IoT) and cloud or edge computing may not have impacted your business strategy, but it may have changed structural aspects of the operations strategy. In defining the business plan, it is important that the full range of infrastructure criteria you define does not unduly constrain your ability to flex. Your overall business strategy must define an acceptable relative time period for responsiveness to major change.

Part of the operations strategy should be to actively reduce the time, difficulty, and expense of structural changes. Factory-as-a-service (FaaS) has evolved as one approach to help manufacturers manage that challenge, but it is hardly mature. Options are business opportunities.

Simultaneously we must create the foundation to quickly develop new capabilities, and significantly, know which capabilities we need, but don't have. Those important competencies will not develop on their own. Tactical thinking and explaining variances from last month contribute nothing to laying that groundwork.

Identify the Capabilities That Matter Tomorrow

The changes impacting manufacturing are coming at us from all directions, more quickly than ever before. Sensors have been around for what feels like forever, but they now massively impact our options and the value we can provide. The transition from manual equipment to computer-controlled equipment has been going on for decades, but the acceleration in what those can enable revolutionizes our world. Five-axis machines and additive manufacturing are just the beginning.

Long generating "small data" used poorly, we have become enamored with the concept of big data. We can now collect, analyze, and adjust designs and performance of our existing products, as well as generate entirely new solutions to problems our markets face. The answers are unending to the often-asked school question, "How will I ever use this math?" The management, quality, and comprehension of data is relevant to the future of any manufacturer. It is fast becoming a basic requirement. What is the real capability that your company must develop to appropriately incorporate data into your future? How will those capabilities and that data move you toward the mission in line with core values?

In identifying the enterprise capabilities most important to building your enduring future, your head has to be up. No one can foresee all aspects of our changing world, but we can ask important questions that provide guidance. Look beyond current markets and customers, beyond current products, and into your value-adding core competencies. If the former all became obsolete today, which of the latter would still provide value?

As I wrote earlier in this chapter: "If your customers' value-adding thinking isn't evolving quickly, you're in a dangerous market. If yours isn't either, you're in a dangerous business."

Innovation often solves problems that only the innovator can voice. The market is the last to request much beyond faster, better, cheaper. Until it says goodbye. Don't count on it to tell you where your focus should be. Again, Henry Ford and Bill Gates served as visionaries who addressed needs customers did not yet know they had. Does your business operating system ensure you recognize important changes and opportunities? Does it build in the strategic flexibility to evaluate and respond to those?

We cannot afford to keep considering humans as skilled at a specific task. Like it or not, the future requires that we work with people who thrive in ambiguity, who demonstrate a passion for lifelong learning, and who want to try new things. Do your target relationships with employees and suppliers reflect that need?

As we identify the enterprise capabilities of tomorrow, we must also recognize those of today that will no longer be relevant. The position of buyer will soon not exist; salesperson is in similar jeopardy. Passing résumés around before deciding whom to interview has been largely replaced by software, impacting entry-level human resource recruiters. The need for proactive communication and planning consistent with core values should not be overlooked. What other changes can you see on the horizon?

As we unwind one set of job responsibilities to build those that enable endurance, we will sometimes make the wrong decision. Or execute the right decision too slowly. Automation may fail us. The fundamentals of trust, respect, and learning from our mistakes will, in the enduring manufacturer, be deeply ingrained. PDCA discipline will be as basic as breathing. Why? Because rapid, effective change requires it.

While the whirling dervish may appear out of control, he is very much in command of his own actions. He relies on his partners to play their roles to perfection. Each owns individual responsibility, while giving up any semblance of control of the group. The fast, circular motions do not lead to vertigo because the movements are carefully orchestrated to prevent it.

All of manufacturing is a choreography. The flows of information, decisions, materials, value, and cash do not happen by accident. They represent the processes you have in place. Too often those processes were not designed with goals beyond task completion in mind, nor as part of closed-loop systems. Mastery of moving quickly and smoothly to create and deliver value will be the standard of the enduring manufacturer. Design capabilities extraordinaire allow you to create and deliver value with minimal waste. Humans make mistakes; great design makes that irrelevant.

None of us can predict the amazingly powerful device that doesn't yet exist, nor the programming language that will shatter current limitations. But if we leave our linear thinking behind and examine the future conceptually, we can see that it is the mind of the person that matters, not what they can produce in their first week of employment. Quit looking at what you wish you had yesterday, and consider instead the kinds of thinking, problem solving, teamwork, ideation, and analysis the next decade will require.

Despite all your efforts on strategic design of proactive systems to facilitate the future, obstacles will exist. The most limiting of those are self-induced. Some will be externally generated, and a handful will be completely unexpected. An enduring manufacturing organization will recognize those impediments and work with appropriate constituencies, guided by an evolving business operating system, design capabilities, and human development, to determine how best to overcome them. Contingency and mitigation are good; prevention is better. Much easier said than done, but it must be done, regardless. Let's control what we can. Often that is our ability to foresee and to respond quickly.

**TRANSITIONING FROM TACTICAL TO
STRATEGIC THINKING: FINAL THOUGHTS**

- If your customers' value-adding thinking isn't evolving quickly, you're in a dangerous market. If yours isn't either, you're in a dangerous business.
- Not every decision is strategic, but every decision should be guided by strategy. The much-discussed concept of alignment requires that.
- An enduring manufacturer is always searching for better ways to create and deliver more value in support of the mission.

Reactionary, tactical thinking should be the exception, not the rule. Mutually finalized strategy and retained line-of-sight deployment processes enable that. Leaders who consistently voice strategic considerations in priorities and decisions propel the organization forward.

Chapter 8

Overcoming Obstacles

Getting out of our own way

While commonly attributed to Mike Tyson, it was heavyweight boxing champ Joe Lewis who first said, "everyone's got a plan until they get hit." Indeed, if you've made progress taking the first seven steps along the path described within this book, you do have a plan and many of the abilities to execute it. But are you ready to get hit?

Quite different from boxing, many of the hits that organizations take originate internally. The external hits—be they recession, pandemic, labor shortage, natural disaster, or competitor actions—get all the attention, but recognizing and eliminating the self-induced blows is most important. By doing that external obstacles become simply bumps in the road.

The five primary sources of self-induced obstacles are:

- Low expectations
- Poor prioritization
- Slow decision-making
- Lack of discipline
- Poor metrics

Low Expectations

The first of these is by far the most limiting to your company's endurance. It is also the least recognized and most widespread. When you look back at the prior chapters you will likely find those expectations have seeped into everything you've identified, except your mission. Our passion is rarely limited by expectations, but our progress toward it certainly is.

I remind you of the words of US President John F Kennedy: "We choose to go to the Moon in this decade and do the other things, not because they are easy, but because they are hard, because that goal will serve to organize and measure the best of our energies and skills, because that challenge is one that we are willing to accept, one we are unwilling to postpone, and one which we intend to win, and the others, too."

It may be tempting to accept average; insisting on greatness can be exhausting. That is one reason why a meaningful mission plays such a crucial role in your future. An enduring manufacturer cannot afford to be satisfied by being better than most. Is your organization as good as it could be? It is your responsibility as the leader to accept the challenge and not postpone it.

I wrote earlier about the critical role of leveraging exceptional design capabilities in building an enduring manufacturing business. If those are used to meet a low standard, they are wasted. If they are not used to figure out how to eliminate conflicting priorities, they're being wasted. Kennedy could have offered twenty years or been willing to let an astronaut die in the effort. He did not. The world is much better because of his high expectations. Your mission will be better served by your high expectations.

The story of Steve Jobs insisting that the first iPhone have a glass screen instead of plastic is well known. What many do not realize is that he made that demand after the product was announced and just five months before shipping to the market was scheduled. He didn't like the scratches that appeared on the plastic screen of the phone after a few days in his pocket. Efforts to convince him it was impossible failed. By cooperating with the R&D team at Corning, the phone was introduced with that glass screen. High expectations, partnerships, and a business operating system that emphasized design extraordinaire enabled that success.

Consider how the unsolvable contradiction between quality and quantity was attacked by Philip Crosby's 1979 book *Quality is Free*. Outstanding design of product and production systems make that a false distinction. Decent design has reduced the contradiction in most manufacturers, but certainly not all. It seems executives think the contradiction has been resolved as long as workers are not constantly asking, "Which do you want? Quality or quantity?" Low expectations.

Some, like Tesla, choose not to focus on quality. Because of Elon Musk's wrong-headed lust for total automation of production, both quantity and quality initially faced significant struggles. While the company's production rates are now higher, quality problems remain. That business chose to shift those issues to its customers rather than use its design capabilities to produce a cost-effective, high-quality vehicle. I remind you that Tesla's mission is to speed the transition to sustainable energy. Apparently, Musk and his executive team believe that passionate customers will accept low quality. Perhaps the speed of conversion to electric vehicles would be greater if solid quality enticed more people to buy them. At least I hope the Tesla team is examining the question.

Failure work is always signaling deficient design of something. Design today may be much improved over yesterday's, and could be better than everyone else's, but if the signal is there, it's inadequate, nonetheless. As you eliminate easily recognized failure work, look for other signals of design weakness. Excess time and cost can be nebulous, but always indicate the potential for improved design. Fifty-percent reductions in both are possible in most every manufacturing business. Focus on reducing time; lower costs will follow.

Consider your own business. Have industry comparisons or profits convinced you the organization has mastered effective design? Is failure work accepted as unavoidable? While some signs of failure are acknowledged in production, does your business measure them outside of there? Even in manufacturing processes, only a few aspects are commonly considered. Scrap and rework data are often collected, with the goal of creating less. But are the product and processes designed together to *prevent* scrap, rework, injuries, field problems, or other failure work? Was your business designed to be profitable, or is that a hoped-for outcome?

Does your new product development (NPD) process produce 100 percent on time and on budget? Do those products serve the market and your mission exceptionally well? Is the need for service and repair activities considered something that should be eliminated by better design? How is product design actively considering potential materials and manufacturability challenges? While DFX is a common concept, in practice it seems to grab only the lowest of fruit.

Professionals claim that target costs and introduction schedules limit what they can design. That is true for product, for production capabilities, and for new concepts. So here we are with another unsolvable contradiction. Instead of quality and quantity, this time it is extraordinary design and perceived costs, with schedules thrown in for good measure.

If we don't have systems and processes that can resolve those conflicts, are we at least working on that instead of simply accepting conditions as insurmountable? In defense industries, usages of manufacturing readiness levels (MRL) and technology readiness levels (TRL) processes and definitions are common. Many outside of defense consider those best practices as well.

Those manufacturers with extraordinary design capabilities are asking and answering MRL/TRL level-two, -three, and -four considerations during level-one activities. They know that preventing failure work, which is created in the early levels, is possible. Even if they haven't yet perfected that thinking—still allowing some technical debt—their lead times and rework in design have been significantly reduced. Only with that expectation is significant reduction in time and cost attained.

Again, Ozgene is one example of a business accepting the challenge and creating amazing success. The organization focuses relentlessly on the concept of time. The company fully understands that most elapsed time does not emanate from value-add steps. One strategic decision was to leverage a cloud-based IT infrastructure designed specifically to eliminate manual handoffs and to speed information flows. Ozgene is designing for scalability. New international sites are integrated quickly.

Look also to your business processes. What could the output be if they were designed exceptionally well? Approval processes are one simple example of an over-used step intended to prevent major errors, but that, in fact, cost time and money. If an organization were to simply examine those to understand what necessitates approvals, it could eliminate or modify most of that and become much more effective.

Think root cause analysis. No one would use root cause to eliminate resource-sucking processes until they are seen as a problem to be solved. Whether considering operations or business processes, it is important to remember that local optimization does not create global optimization. Always take a system view as you design or improve processes. Constant attention to high expectations makes a big difference. Those expectations must cross the business, not simply task accomplishment.

In 2004, *IndustryWeek* magazine published an article on the one-day close. It asked what that financial department goal really meant in practice. My included input was that the phrase is a euphemism for timely and believable data. A company that takes longer than "immediate" to accomplish the monthly financial process of closing the books clearly is operating without those. By setting the expectation of an immediate financial close, many data problems had to be resolved. Significant wasted time and, of course, failure work had to be eliminated.

The sad implication of that is that others did not have good information at hand either. Technology helped with speed, but it didn't resolve many accuracy challenges. Completely accurate inventory remains a rarity. Finance is happy with an inventory valuation that is close to what the books show, but operations has a very different need for *what/where/how many* information. What expectation is set at your company? Are your processes designed to generate that output?

Learning what does not work is valuable. But only if, once learned, it is consistently integrated into design thinking. Understanding the attributes of the scenarios in which it doesn't work is even more valuable, as it enables your team to learn and apply even more. That learning can drastically cut the time it takes to develop new products and new processes. Are you expecting product and process development to take less and less time with better and better results? Again, I ask, are your processes designed to enable that?

I've been told by more than one manufacturing executive that I just don't understand how difficult their business is. In many cases, I don't. But what is really important is that, while I never accept complexity as hopeless, many leaders do. I'm not suggesting that anyone minimize challenges, just that we build a business that is constantly recognizing, anticipating, and overcoming them.

Why did we need Philip Crosby to give us a wake-up call? Apply that same level of expectations to every process in your business. Yes, people make mistakes, but it is only design governed by low expectations that considers human error an inescapable weakness.

Take a look at the enterprise capabilities, the relationships, and the strategy deployment processes you considered in earlier chapters. Challenge the expectations you set there. Can you do something important differently to better serve your mission?

It is unreasonable to expect greatness while doing little to support attaining it. A leader expecting no scrap, no injuries, no failing products, strategic understanding and alignment, competitive superiority, and more—without providing the environment in which those things become possible—is delusional. Their organization will suffer as a result. In building an enduring manufacturing business, we cannot enable low expectations, or a lack of commitment to change them, to be an obstacle to progress. If we know why, we can figure out how. We must ensure our business operating system and commitment to people and design prioritize those efforts and build in success potential (Figure 8.1).

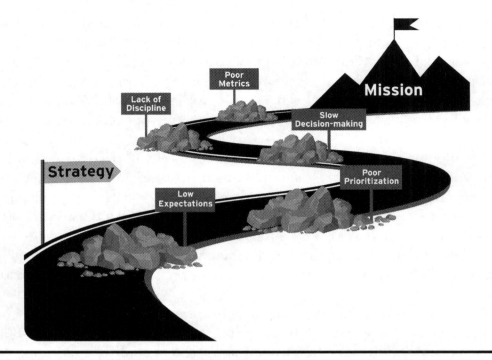

Figure 8.1   Common Self-Induced Obstacles

Poor Prioritization

Manufacturers can get better at absolutely everything. The more expectations rise, the more overwhelming that fact can feel. Leaders have the tools
to manage that, not by reducing expectations, but by defining priorities.
Do not refuse to make the hard decisions of priority setting out of fear that
lower-priority items will not be addressed. That concern should be replaced
with confidence that resources are focused on the most important challenges
and opportunities. Isn't that the purpose of strategy?

There can only be one top priority. There can only be one next-high-
est priority. As described in Chapter 3, the priorities were crystal clear at
Stouffer's. Quality, the customer, and then cost. The many projects that we
undertook were prioritized accordingly. We had just as many balls to toss
into the air as did any other company, but clear priorities made that so much
easier. We focused on completing projects quickly and effectively. That
meant not starting new ones until resources were ready. That's a simple concept that leaders cannot afford to ignore.

The Factory Physics® factual relationships defined by Little's Law and
Kingman's equation are valid in all aspects of workflow and are amazingly

valuable to manufacturing executives in priority setting. While Factory Physics® offers much more, just understanding and applying these two concepts accelerates effective productivity throughout the organization.

Little's Law simply states the mathematical relationship among work in process (WIP), lead time, and throughput. WIP can refer to products under development, active software projects, or customer approvals in progress. The math abides. The bottom line is that the more priorities you insist be pursued at once, the longer it takes any one of them to be accomplished. Effectively, multiple priorities increase WIP—and therefore lead time—while doing nothing to enhance throughput.

Kingman's equation offers mathematical proof of the exponential relationship between utilization, lead time, and variability. As utilization, whether of equipment or a person, approaches 100 percent, lead time increases exponentially. Putting more work on a resource than it can handle (load exceeds capacity) will increase lead time. Forcing that resource to constantly react to changing priorities without processes to eliminate changeover time wastes capacity.

You can look for the mathematical proof of each of these, or simply accept the work others have done as valid. It is. Each of these is lived in every aspect of every manufacturing organization. The leader who can make the tough decisions about priorities will have a very positive impact on the organization. "I want it all and I want it now" precipitates getting very little. "I want this most and that second most" leads to much better outcomes.

I can hear you pointing out that different priorities can take different resources, so multiple priorities are allowed. Well, sort of. There can only be one top organizational priority. There can be a second priority that moves forward to the degree that it takes entirely different resources. I am not suggesting the entire organization only work on one thing at a time. What I am saying is that the entire organization must have clear direction on what takes priority of any shared resource and that all resources be managed at significantly below 100 percent.

The strategy deployment processes described in Chapter 6 are designed to integrate strategic priorities into the thinking of the entire organization, along with clear and constant connection. Any plan poorly communicated or ignored gives rise to confusion over what is most important. Tactical operations can easily focus on increasing measured efficiencies at the cost of what the entire organization agreed to do. The drive toward maximizing efficiencies too often misses the point. Efficiency does not create endurance.

To get anything accomplished, effective leadership will not dump everything on the organization and hope that the resources can sort out what to work on when. That would lead to massive WIP of work elements through-out, and resultant long lead times. Those long lead times lead to expediting, which leads to unpredictable lead times for everything. And all that leads to a frustrated organization that makes no one happy. A well-deployed strategy has provided clear priorities that withstand daily push and pull; otherwise, the plan itself is meaningless.

While Jack Welch's forced ranking of employees to decide whom to fire was misguided, a forced ranking of the potential priorities of your organiza-tion is required. By starting any one of them only when resources are avail-able to process it, the most important items will be completed first. Think of it as a process kanban system. Kanban is both an inventory control and scheduling tool. That workflow design is effective in creating predictable output in product development, as it is in many production environments. It is not the only approach, but it is one well known.

The thinking also provides the flexibility to shift lower-level priorities as the environment changes without disrupting the organization. We learn with time. Our view of the future was imperfect. Simply input the next priority project instead of the one that months ago you thought would have gone next. The concept of "start as late as possible" is a good one for this very reason. That applies to new product development, production orders, accounting processes, and more. The really nice thing about applying Little's Law and Kingman's equation to manage WIP and throughput is that it enhances flexibility while reducing failure work.

Leaders want progress on all things important and to worry less about daily fires. But daily fires are often the result of hectic changes respond-ing to today's call. Today's call may well have been from the leader who fails to understand the impact of their meddling. Their question may be mistakenly implemented as an order and internalized as another change in priorities. Poor prioritization can be imagined from imperfect com-munication or can be very real. In either case, leader behavior is at the root. Take the time for clarity; priorities are too important to be taken for granted.

Slow Decision-Making

Expectations and prioritization are both decisions. Neither is composed of easy questions, but it is the responsibility of the leader to define both. As we all know, "that's why you get the big bucks!"

Strategy decisions belong to leaders as well, with both horizontal and vertical input from the organization. Some of these high-level decisions will be good ones, and others not so good. The ones that turn out to be wrong must be recognized as such quickly and corrected effectively; they impact the entire organization and likely all its constituencies as well. Again, a designed trigger system can be productive here. Egos cannot be allowed to interfere with those activities.

If those decisions have been made well, quickly, and communicated clearly, you're still not off the hook. Thousands of decisions are made daily throughout the entire business microclimate; the better and faster those are made, the better the health of that overall system. So why is slow decision-making a significant, self-inflicted obstacle? Because many decisions involve extensive elapsed time, rely on bad information, or are poorly thought through.

Now that's a heck of a criticism. I wouldn't make it if I hadn't seen evidence in literally hundreds of companies across the spectrum of manufacturing industries, sizes, and markets. It's certainly not from lack of available information about how to make decisions. There are three, four, five, or six types of decisions depending on what you read; there is equally divergent information about styles and methods. I invite you to check out that kind of information at your leisure.

The obstacles from slow decision-making most relevant to this discussion emanate from *who* and *when*.

The stronger the framework for identifying and building enterprise capabilities, the faster and better decisions will be made within appropriate time frames by appropriate people. Without agreement on both the who and when, decision-making can be what stands between your organization and the capabilities it must master. This includes decisions made by external constituencies that impact your performance. How often does your team wait until the next weekly, monthly, or even less-frequent meeting to bring an issue to the attention of those who can address it?

Just as your company is not an island, neither are decisions made within the microclimate formed by you and your constituencies. Slow customer responses? Suppliers delaying communication of problems? Employees making childcare decisions in weather events or school closings? The decisions they make, or fail to make, can impact the total system. You cannot allow your business to consider itself the victim of all those decisions. These are examples of predictable decisions that you can choose to accept as insurmountable obstacles, or choose to design for.

Want speed and agility? Invest a day or two simply observing work; really observing it. Gaining permission, double-checking, doing more analysis, and continuing workarounds are common impediments to those targeted characteristics. When I wrote earlier about the quality, cost, and time elements designed into your processes, these are examples most can relate to. Your processes must include steps to identify and eliminate these frustrating but low-profile obstacles. While the search for perfection can drive your organization, the search for perfect information can cripple it.

Risk tolerance certainly is a factor, but one frequently overrated. How does the downside of a particular wrong—but fast—decision offset the potential development of the person or improvement of the system generating it? Every decision should include a quick upside/downside thought process, but most can be done in under a second. All of your constituencies must understand your risk tolerance as an organization, and how the speed of their decision-making is likely to impact microclimate success. The more agile the organization, the easier it is to predict the future well enough.

Deciding whether to ship product on time, but without the customer-required label, (a) points out an operational system weakness, and (b) should be answered by the business operating system. Not specifically, but generically. Shipping personnel should not have to call a supervisor, sales, or customer service to make that decision. Furthermore, the fact that it happens should drive review of the relevant systems for improvement.

Effective design proactively prevents problems; effective problem solving reactively eliminates them. The former best supports the intentions of enduring manufacturing businesses; the latter provides improvement until improved system design is a priority. By paying attention to the types and frequency of decisions that should not be required at all, design weaknesses can be identified and addressed. One reason kanban is so popular is because that scheduling and inventory control system reduces the need to hunt for the supervisor to decide what to work on next. Design the system to provide good answers immediately.

I see leaders increasingly moving toward building consensus before making a decision. I also see executive fingers stuck in lower-level decisions. I see second guessing, failure to delegate, and lack of respect for both time and downside/upside thinking. Consensus isn't a bad thing, unless it slows decision-making beyond its value. In some cases, the leader simply needs to make the decision and worry about selling it later. If lower-level people—the ones who actually do the work—are not able to make decisions that their jobs require, fix that. An operator searching for a supervisor or a quality tech to get a question answered is an opportunity to examine why the system is designed to necessitate that.

Automation offers the potential to take repeated and rules-driven decisions off the human plate. Robotic process automation (RPA) is a description of a category of tools to do just that, primarily with office activities. IIoT can automate many decisions—made and executed in nanoseconds. That family of technologies can also support providing accurate, timely information to the place where it is needed for decision-making by a person.

If decisions take too long in your organization, observe first who is involved in making them. That aspect of your business operating system or process design should be improved to reduce the number. Can any be automated because the answer is rules-based? Which ones are driven by lack of available information and how can processes make that data available both when and where the decisions get made? Or can we design the requirement for the decision out of the process? A fully capable process does not require asking if the customer will accept the flaw.

The biggest challenge to faster decision-making is lack of trust. If making lower-level decisions is taking any of your time, you have not yet fulfilled your basic responsibility: to create the environment in which people succeed. It's time to be clear on the goal of the process, ensure the process is capable of producing that output, train people on the process, and then capture feedback on any flaws in the process to improve it. Leadership owns the rules and the tools and is responsible for the success of the people. If you have to be involved in making detailed decisions, look in the mirror.

Lack of Discipline

Every leader of a manufacturing business should be familiar with the work of W. Edwards Deming. If you're not, please learn about him soon. His advice was simple, brilliant, and is praised to this day. Those who are disappointed using it, or deny his fourteen points, generally aren't interested in the behavior changes necessitated. Discipline is the most common failing. Failing to find something better, many companies now turn back to his teachings.

As is true for all of us, Deming stood upon the shoulders of his predecessors. He studied the work of Walter Shewhart, the early quality guru. Deming was instrumental in the turnaround of Japan after World War II, both because of his statistical demonstrations that design for quality reduces costs, and because the Japanese leadership listened to him. He didn't share with them anything he hadn't told American business, but domestic corporate leaders believed they couldn't benefit from his advice. Japan passed us by in many industries in under a decade. If there is anything specific about the Japanese culture that differentiates it, discipline might be it.

PDCA is the well-known initialism for the Shewhart-Deming process for making improvements. It began as plan-do-check-act, but Deming later changed the initialism to PDSA—the S standing for study—as he observed too many people thinking *check* and *inspection* are synonymous. This simple-to-understand, but apparently difficult-to-live concept would propel most manufacturing businesses light years ahead of where they are now.

The only real difficulty is in the discipline it requires to be effective. *Plan* seems fairly straightforward, but it apparently is not. Shortcuts are common.

Consider the Great American Kaizen Event. Most manufacturers using this methodology *plan* very little, complete a bit of *do*, do little *checking*, and often intentionally ignore *act* (or *adjust*). We're in a hurry to move on to the next process before actually making a real difference in this first one. If your organization doesn't have time to learn, reexamine priorities.

Consider how the process of PDCA, which is what the kaizen event is intended to follow, should work. For those larger challenges, really good companies may plan for weeks or months. They have a clear definition of the problem to be solved or opportunity to be leveraged. Improvement metrics are not guesses or hopes, and instead are well-defined expectations. Assignments may be to figure out how to reduce by one person the manpower required to generate the same level of output; figure out how to reduce the space required by 50 percent; figure out how to reduce change-over times by 75 percent.

The Toyota truck factory in San Antonio, Texas, plans and executes rolling model-year changes. This typically involves hundreds of new and eliminated parts and work instructions. Needed changes to part presentation and supplies, to work instructions, and relevant quality processes are planned in detail. The changes are implemented as the production line carries the new model to each workstation, with all the options it may offer, with no production stoppage. This process may be a year in planning, a few hours in implementation, weeks in checking, and myriad more hours improving the system through adjustments both immediately and as part of ongoing continuous improvement activities.

Needed improvements from the kaizen event should be implemented quickly, without the Friday-morning punch list most kaizen events count on. Then undertake verification of how the change impacted the targets, looking for any negative or positive unintended consequences. That check (study) phase may take minutes, hours, days, or months, depending on the complexity of the changes. This is where we can learn from the thinking used in the plan stage. You are now in position to make further adjustments, if appropriate. Better is always possible; priorities will determine the timing.

The process I've just described requires a great deal more discipline than does the Monday–Friday do-what-you-can approach, and also enables meaningful, effective change. Making changes to an unstable process is an entirely different ballgame. Process capability should be known, whether in a production or an office environment. It may be better to target a specified reduction in variability within a process than to make more visibly obvious changes. That's basically the intention of six sigma methodologies.

A manufacturing business cannot develop and maintain critical enterprise capabilities without discipline. PDCA is a great concept that many claim to utilize, but few actually do. A robust PDCA process for making changes is one of the most powerful competencies an organization can develop. The lack of discipline in following defined processes, in planning and executing change, in simply doing what you say you will do, will preclude endurance. Discipline does not mean harsh or rigid. It does mean complying with guidance and rules so that we can learn. We are disciplined when we drive, when we stand in a line, or when we want to become better. If we are not disciplined in those common scenarios, chaos emerges.

It sounds much easier than it apparently is: do what you say you will do, follow processes and rules, and follow through with others on anything important. Perseverance does not imply a lack of trust; it implies significance. Lack of discipline, experienced as lack of interest in pursuing, means lack of learning; lack of learning means no endurance. That is much too big a price to pay.

Poor Metrics

The fifth primary source of internally generated obstacles to building a successful and enduring manufacturing business is metrics: the lack of good ones; an emphasis on bad ones.

How can you tell the difference? The realized benefit from having the information has to more than exceed the cost of getting the information. If that's not the case, there's a problem.

Do you have obligatory metrics, those that every manufacturer seems to think are important? Examples include equipment utilization and labor efficiency. Both of those are more likely to drive bad decisions than good ones.

Managers often want equipment utilization to be high, or at least higher than it is. Equipment should be used when it is needed and not when it is not. Absorbing overhead is a silly reason to increase utilization. Kingman's equation was already offered.

Similarly, supervisors often believe that employees reporting time against a work order or a quantity of production allows them to know who is a good worker and who is not. Worse than silly, that is dangerous. That reporting costs money, and it does not measure the worker. The worker is limited by process performance. Measure that, not individuals. Job costing is equally misleading.

Productivity is defined as output divided by input. You know what you ship, and you know what payroll is. There you have it: the labor productivity of the business. Similar, simple metrics can be defined to measure process productivity or variability.

After the many misguided obligatory metrics come the equally useless, untimely, inaccurate records. If a report doesn't improve the quality of decisions, why incur the cost of generating and reviewing it? Most accounting falls into this category. Have you ever said, "I can't make that decision until I get the dispatch from accounting?" Unlikely. Do what the law requires. Don't use late, poor-quality metrics to make decisions, no matter how many digits to the right of the decimal point are reported. Precision and accuracy are two entirely different things.

The third popular category of poor metrics is that which doesn't provide clear, unambiguous interpretation. If the response to your follow-up question is "it depends," the metric is not a good one. "It depends on mix" is a common indicator of a poorly defined metric.

Before going crazy defining your KPIs, be crystal clear on which are leading indicators, and which merely measure results. It is obviously important to know results, but that doesn't tell you what went wrong or right—merely that something did. Even those have to be timely and accurate to be helpful. Worthwhile metrics are visual, available real time, and located at the point where relevant decision-making typically occurs.

To examine your metrics and change them for the better, consider these questions:

- Can you describe in some detail one or more decisions that you will make differently depending on the value of the metric? If you can't, the number you are spending resources to track is perhaps interesting, but irrelevant.
- Which decisions require knowing the value of a metric before you can wisely make them? Do the metrics you use for that provide the clarity you need?
- Does the value of better decisions made possible only with the help of the metric outweigh the costs of obtaining and reporting the metric?

Collecting data for analysis to use in making process changes is different from metrics used to run your business. True KPIs help you run your business better. If you would have made the same decision regardless of the value of the metric, it is not paying for itself.

We all know the trick to reducing workload: quit sending a report and see who notices. Too many metrics are reviewed by habit, not to improve decision-making. That's a costly routine that should be broken. If you want to improve efficiency, eliminating poor metrics is a good place to start.

Yes, There Are More

Seeing what is right under our noses is often our biggest challenge.

Building an enduring business is difficult enough without tripping over self-induced obstacles. By getting out of our own way, the organization is a much healthier place and a much better business. Frustrations, confusion, and boredom are great indications of opportunity. Certainly, some of each of those are born outside your company, but you rarely need to look beyond the microclimate of your business constituencies. That chaos theory butterfly is not your biggest threat. Self-induced obstacles are common. The best news is that you have everything you need to remove them.

Yes, you should also look externally for signals to enable better circumstances for all. In addressing these internal obstacles, you will also reduce those generated from outside your organization. You are not the victim of either your customers or any of your other constituents, unless you choose to be. And you certainly do not want them to be victimized by you.

Every obstacle can be heightened by an organizational structure that makes it more difficult to identify and overcome. No business succeeds because of its organizational structure, but structure can impact success significantly. Silos are given much of the blame, and rightfully so. Some businesses are best served by siloed organizations; most are not. Organizational structure is a choice. There are many to choose from and many more you could design to enhance the endurance of your manufacturing business. The immediate challenge is to define the optimal structure for your business today.

OVERCOMING OBSTACLES: FINAL THOUGHTS

■ By recognizing and eliminating self-induced obstacles, you will convert external obstacles into mere bumps in the road.

■ Our passion is rarely limited by low expectations, but our progress toward it certainly is.

■ Leaders have the tools to manage the many demands on the business, not by reducing expectations, but by defining priorities.

Which of the five common self-induced obstacles described in this chapter is limiting organizational progress the most in your business? Choose a single step and begin diminishing that impediment.

Chapter 9

Strategy Defines Organization

An organization chart can support the endurance of a business, or amplify weaknesses

Except in farm country, "silos" is a dirty word. As well it should be. Yet it seems to describe the most common organizational structure we see in manufacturing businesses.

Companies are often organized by skill set or primary tasks, not by authority or decision-making responsibilities. Structures rarely are designed to instill core values or magnify human potential. In larger companies, they often take the form of silos within siloed strategic business units (SBUs). When one business unit sells products or services to another, that structure can create nasty fights over transfer pricing. When they are entirely separate businesses with no cross sales, valuable knowledge and resources are rarely, if ever, effectively shared. I experienced both realities when I was a division leader for TRW Inc. My first responsibilities were to resolve the transfer pricing challenge, and then entice multiple plants to coordinate metals supplies and expertise. Poor metrics and contradictory incentives precluded such cooperation.

There are options.

Learning from Others

One important place to leverage your design capabilities is in defining accountabilities and responsibilities for every aspect of the organization. Structures that complexify decision-making and instantiate leadership ambiguity can stop progress dead in its tracks. Once again, understanding why you have the structure you have—and why a different structure might better support building endurance—is a great place to start. And no single structure should be believed eternally optimal.

As with most design, there is little need to start from a blank sheet of paper. By examining a handful of notable organizations, we can gain a view into what can work, what likely won't, and the whys of each. Apple, 3M, and Zappos are just a few of the many from whom we can learn valuable lessons. None of those is a silver bullet for you, but each is a goldmine of thinking.

When Steve Jobs returned to Apple in 1997, the organization had a structure common for businesses of its size. It was divided into market-facing SBUs, each with its own P&L, its own general manager, its own team of hardware and software experts, and its own set of overhead support. Upon resuming the CEO role, Jobs immediately put the organization under one P&L, eliminated the roles of those running SBUs, and created a more traditional functional organization.

What makes the new structure different from most is that the functions were aligned with control of expert decision-making. The hardware group makes hardware decisions; the software group makes software decisions. The organization continues to evolve as technology evolves, but not away from this basic functional, expertise-based, decision-control concept.

The thinking that underlies that company's structure can apply to many. For Apple it is from knowing that in a rapidly changing world of technology, only those with the deepest understanding of any aspect of it have the knowledge to make decisions in their arena: hardware experts for hardware, software for software, AI for AI. But acknowledging that the structure is more broadly effective, marketing makes marketing decisions, design makes design decisions, and retail makes retail decisions. These arenas of functional expertise do not operate as silos in the "throw it over the wall" sense. Communication and expectations are effective, and decisions reside with those best able to make them. Collaborative debate is integral to the BOS.

In most large companies, the "general" in general manager is emphasized. At Apple, there are no general managers in any intention of the phrase. Leaders invest most of their time in learning and owning—very little in delegating. They must have expertise in their areas of responsibility, which explains the attention to learning. Few mid-size manufacturers rely on leaders actually learning and gaining new expertise; even fewer large ones do. If the executive team of an organization believes it has all the expertise it will ever need, endurance is not within the realm of possibility.

Many believe that CEO Tim Cook does not have the passion for products that Steve Jobs did. They find him a fine CEO, but not a fine visionary leader. That is not a weakness in the structure, but an organizational need to be met. Apple has a design group that makes design decisions, but that is not the same as the passion for a product from the top. It is interesting to watch how an entirely new product family will be born. Not an iWatch, an iPad, an iPod, a laptop, or a desktop, but an entirely new means of enriching people's daily lives. That is the purpose of Apple; they will see something the rest of us cannot and make it happen.

Your business likely does not face such revolutionary change within the technologies integral to your product, but that doesn't relegate this concept to the trash heap. The thinking of aligning decision-making with those best qualified to understand and make specific decisions is difficult to reject out of hand. Most manufacturers expect the product manager role to make decisions that they are not the most qualified to make. With a short-term focus on profitability driving many of those decisions, important advances are unlikely. It is worth thinking about how your current structure assigns responsibilities for the multiplicity of decisions in your organization, and how it may undermine any "giant leap for mankind."

Restructuring is a really nasty word to most employees of large manufacturers, because it's typically a euphemism for significant layoffs. Many are desperate attempts to rearrange the Titanic's deck chairs, long missing the real value of effective structure, strategy, and planning. A structure that supports the strategy should be reviewed when strategy changes significantly. Structure should be reviewed if it has not been effective in building the enterprise capabilities that matter. Changing the organizational chart primarily as a cost reduction method signals desperation.

3M is highly regarded for its approach to innovation and innovative thinking throughout the organization. Even they, like all of us, should regularly reevaluate structure. In early 2020, that business announced a reorganization that involved a relatively small reduction in force—unless you were one of those impacted—but significantly, aligned with a new operating model that changed how and where decisions are made.

Priorities that had been determined by geographic leadership are now transitioned into one of four pre-existing SBUs, down from five in 2018. Some functions, such as manufacturing, supply chain, and customer experience, have become enterprise wide, in the announced hope of gaining efficiencies. I have to admire 3M leadership for seeing the value in giving operations responsibility for end-to-end customer value provision. As I described in Chapter 7, input from commercial and finance sectors of the business will be critical to success. This part of the structure and responsibility changes is a great step forward.

Top executives claim that this reorganization is integral to a key element—transformation—of their overriding strategy. 3M appears committed to its SBU model for now, believing that is how it can best serve various markets and drive effective innovation. They will have plenty of opportunities to assess how well this continuing division works for each of its five constituencies, if they choose to examine all five. Perhaps they will learn from Apple. But perhaps the organization's goods and services are so disconnected from one another that the Apple structure offers no value. A pure conglomerate lends itself to the SBU model, but other than to make money, is there any reason to own disconnected organizations? How are each of the constituencies benefited by that financial model?

The Amazon-owned, online shoe retailer Zappos began rolling out holacracy as its organizational structure in 2013. That amorphous approach is really very little structure at all. Then-CEO Tony Hsieh described it as without hierarchy, managers, or titles. He believed this freedom would work amazingly well for all five constituencies, but knew that not every individual would like it. Almost one in five employees decided to accept the 2015 offered buyout intended for those who wanted more structure than holacracy would offer.

Zappos' transition to holacracy has certainly had growing pains, which is what Hsieh was trying to avoid. He saw that traditional structures did not scale well and believed that this model would better support significant growth. The company, known for amazing customer service, became internally focused as it transitioned. Customers noticed. Zappos has since brought back manager roles, along with other changes. Recently, the business had over 400 team circles and almost 5000 related roles—numbers that ebb and flow as ideas do.

Perhaps a more gradual approach to these very dramatic changes in responsibilities and work content would have helped more employees adapt and succeed. Hsieh could have considered the slower 3M approach to major change; maybe 3M learned from watching Zappos.

As I wrote in Chapter 1, "Reacting with an on/off mindset—changing everything or changing nothing—fails without exception. Go fast, but not too fast." In his passion, Hsieh appeared to shoot right past that sweet spot of fast enough, but not too fast. While holacracy has not been proven a failure, using the on/off switch to move to it has one important data point against it. Sometimes jumping in the deep end works; sometimes it does not. But again, it would be shortsighted to toss out the concept because of a single data point. There remains much to be learned. Sitting back saying "I knew it wouldn't work" reflects a culture of judgement and right and wrong, not one of innovation or learning. Endurance requires different thinking than that.

In deciding which organizational structure is best for your business today, ask why structure matters at all. Is it not just a necessary evil that doesn't really matter? The short answer is no.

It must support strategy development, communication, and execution, and also reflect the needs of the current plan to move the entire organization toward the mission and vision. It must augment expression of core values and development of enterprise capabilities as those needs evolve. It must support creation and delivery of amazing value to the markets while generating strategic profits. It is a strategic choice and should not simply default to "what we've always done."

The Circle Organization Structure

Let's consider a first step that Zappos could have taken on the way, or not, to holacracy. I'm not a fan of holacracy in its complete form, but many of the concepts have value. Learning leaders do not reject entire ideas just because aspects of one failed in a specific circumstance.

The total lack of structure, defined leadership roles, and communication appear to have been the biggest weaknesses. Let's take a moment to consider a form that retains those missing elements while leveraging the positive aspects of the thinking. I will focus on operations for this example.

For visual simplicity, Figure 9.1 shows operations as having one overall leader, with four executives or managers reporting to her. Each of those four have defined areas of responsibilities and direct reports. The circle comes into play to reflect how the individual resources are used, developed, and coordinated.

For purposes of convenience, let's call the four areas of responsibility customer, product development, supply chain and production, and technology, led by Harry, Sue, Bill, and Mary, respectively. Each leader has a team of workers (indicated by H, S, B, or M in the figure) for whom they have success responsibility, regardless of work assignments. Each leader serves as the primary leadership contact for those same people outside of project-related decisions. Project teams hold responsibility for projects.

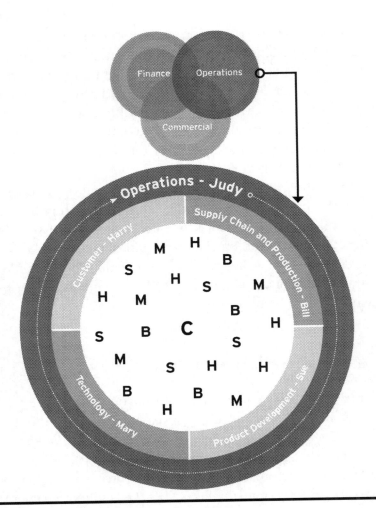

Figure 9.1   Circle Organization Structure

As any problem or project arises, the four managers and the operations leader review its significance and who should serve on the team address-ing it. A central operations coordinator (indicated by the C) tracks which employees are serving on which project teams and why. Together they consider personal development plans, specialties, other project assignments, and risk, and talk with the candidates to ensure a good fit for all. Individual assignments cross boundaries regularly. A poor selection does not work for anyone, and no one is motivated to support such a choice. When a team problem is identified, members and managers work together to resolve it. The objectives are aligned.

The employees and their managers have responsibility for individual and team success, which then creates organizational success. All of this is done within the context of the mission, vision, core values, enterprise capabilities, and the current strategy.

A business could implement this approach one subarea at a time, one primary group—e.g., operations, as in this example—at a time, or the entire company at once. I believe the last option listed should be the last option considered, as it is the most significant level of change impacting the most people all at the same time. Call that the Zappos all-in approach, with important refinements.

I encourage beginning any conversion to this kind of structure one subgroup at a time, beginning with one of your more mature groups. Let's use technology as our pilot operations subgroup. Mary might have three primary areas of responsibility under technology, and each of her direct reports (indicated by an M) has some level of expertise in at least one of those three. They will work on projects that enable experience in, for example, supply chain and production, just as product development team members will. This system facilitates the growth of every employee.

The managers will also lead and participate in projects outside their areas of responsibility, preparing them for greater contribution to the whole. As more groups, and then commercialization and finance are brought into this approach, it is easy to see how succession planning is built in.

Decision-making is not aligned in the same expert-based approach that Apple offers, nor necessarily in the mix of 3M's SBU and shared services model. Each of those models can build in succession planning just as well as this circular model, if that is emphasized. The best model depends on your devotion to breadth versus depth of experience, as well as expertise in grooming new leaders. Any structure you choose must make clear when and by whom decisions are made, and where accountabilities lie.

In the effort of implementing a subgroup structure, you will discover what types of organizational changes your leaders, managers, and employees are ready to take on, and are prepared to lead successfully. You can observe personal and organizational characteristics that support—and those that hinder—this approach. Learning from one subgroup can prepare additional groups for success if and as you decide to deploy this structure further.

Additionally, as more groups are included in this organizational view, each employee could benefit from enhanced development, communication, and insights into how the company actually works. If the manufacturer chooses this structure for the entire business with three large circles—one for operations, one for commercial, and one for finance—it enables breadth or depth to the potential benefits as employees are included in projects in the other sectors. Those three circles could show intersections, like a traditional Venn diagram, where cross-fertilization is encouraged.

Designing Optimal Structure

There is no reason why the entire organization has to operate in a single, identical structure. Remember the current 3M approach—a mix of SBU with several significant cross-company shared services. What is important is that the full organization understands how it works and is free to suggest improvements and point out weaknesses.

The only reason to choose the circular structure is because you believe it will better serve in accomplishing your mission and vision consistent with core values, building enterprise competencies, and executing a well-defined strategy. If you believe your current structure, or a different one, is better for all of that, by all means do not move to this circle-based structure. That advice is good for any structure you might consider. Please, remember at all times that structure is a fluid, strategic choice, with effectiveness criteria built into your business operating system.

You could consider this structure as creating "employees without borders." As leaders are brought into this same assignment of responsibilities, it becomes "leaders without borders." That does not imply constant change, nor a lack of clarity. It does indicate flexibility and agility that might be extremely important to your mission and strategy.

Many "executive development" programs for high-potential, fresh college graduates are based on an "expose widely before assigning specifically" thought process. If you believe that propels them faster toward success, why limit that program to the chosen few? And why insist they be assigned a single functional role when the two years is up?

Just as none of us could be picked up and plopped on Mars without some preparation, do not expect your managers or employees to come to work Monday ready for major organizational changes. Prepare them to succeed. They can if you do.

As you consider various structures, you will probably discover that many of your human resource (HR) policies were designed for a specific approach and do not support other options well. Compensation is the most obvious, but there are others. Job descriptions, hiring, and disciplinary processes may well need to be adjusted as well.

The annual evaluation has never been an effective means to develop employees, although is frequently described as having that purpose. As a former executive who had to document and discuss those evaluations with peers, HR, and the employees themselves, as well as be on the receiving end, I attest to the lack of actual value. In the more than thirty years I have been consulting, nothing has provided evidence to the contrary, though there are likely a few exceptions. The annual process builds in hurried thinking, "what have you done for me lately" summaries, and little meaningful attention to employee growth.

Delegation of responsibility for professional development to the employee is based on theory that may simply miss the point. It is not a game of hot potato. It is not that you, the manager, or they, the employee, must own and execute it. Growth is in everyone's best interest. Cannot the entire organization support the interests and potential of each employee? Ongoing scheduled conversations can overcome those limitations. Rapid learning cycles are all the rage in product development, but don't apply elsewhere?

While no structure precludes meaningful employee development efforts, some simplify them. But there is much more to designing and living an effective organizational structure. If your current structure in no way interferes with the execution of your strategy and supports everything else that you need from it, move on. If not, perhaps a tweak is all that is needed. At least ask the questions openly and honestly and consider the possibilities. Structure is likely not a primary strength, but it can well be a weakness.

STRATEGY DEFINING ORGANIZATION: FINAL THOUGHTS

- Organizational structure is a strategic choice and should not simply default to "what we've always done."
- Companies are often organized by skill set or primary tasks, not by authority or decision-making responsibilities. Structures rarely are designed to instill core values or magnify human potential.
- If the executive team of an organization believes it has all the expertise it will ever need, endurance is not within the realm of possibility. Intentional, lifelong learning should be designed in.

Understanding why you have the current organizational structure—and why a different structure might better facilitate endurance—is a great place to start.

Chapter 10

The Evergreen Manufacturer Begets the Evergreen Customer

Top of value, care, mind, reliability, and experience does the trick

Building any business is difficult. Building a successful *and* enduring manufacturing business is not more difficult, but it is different. It involves not *more* work, but *better* work that is more fun and creates meaning. The path is not a cafeteria from which you can grab whatever looks good. Given that your business already exists, you will probably not start with the first step and follow them in sequence in taking action. But you should consider and prioritize each and every one and do so regularly. No steps are optional. Financial viability is, of course, what makes all else possible. Here we are focusing on the differentiators of building manufacturing businesses that last.

Enduring Growth and Dangerous Growth

Growth is a requirement of endurance. Not the traditional focus on financial growth, which is more likely to sound the death knell of a manufacturer. Personal growth for you—the leader—and every employee. Relationship growth with all five constituencies. Progress toward the mission. Growth in the value your organization provides to its markets. Growth of capabilities, of thinking, or even into identifying a more evolved mission.

Many look down on people living paycheck to paycheck, yet many companies do the same thing. We seem to think that liquid reserves are being wasted; that we should be investing everything in expanding the business. That reasoning contributed significantly to the numerous bankruptcies and shutdowns that occurred during the pandemic and during recessions. Looking for root cause, those behaviors stem from the conviction that financial growth is the goal, and anything not focused on increasing sales and market share misses the point.

Building a manufacturing business to endure takes something very different.

The United States as a country is about 250 years old. Our wild-west mentality leads us to tear down homes and buildings to replace them with something bigger and more modern. Working for others has been so unpleasant that our children would often prefer to build their own company than continue an existing one. The obsessive pursuit of wealth is not limited to America, but our demonstrated interpretation of capitalism is that people get what they deserve. Our long-term view is perhaps five years at best.

Businesses that endure focus on ensuring the future, not on building a bigger today. Perhaps that distinction is why so few manufacturing businesses do stand the test of time.

In Japan, the view of the future is much bigger than a person, or a person's lifetime. It is no surprise then that the country is home to more than 33,000 businesses older than one hundred years. Japan certainly does not have all the answers, nor does Africa, Europe, or North America. The point is to learn from everywhere and everyone. The Asian islands that comprise Japan are home to businesses over 500 years old, and amazingly, a handful that claim to have been in continuous operation for over 1,000 years. Nintendo, which sounds to my baby boomer ears like a young company, is approaching the age of 150.

During my first trip to Europe, I was enthralled by centuries-old churches and buildings. I had previously visited Chaco Canyon, the ancestral home of North American Pueblo peoples, but somehow caves in cliff walls didn't seem as exciting. Since then, I've visited Jordan, Israel, and Egypt, better internalizing the creative genius of those before me. It is much easier to build something that stands for a decade, or even a few, than to build something that endures.

Building an Enduring Manufacturing Business

The biggest distinction of long-lasting businesses is not new product development or go-to-market strategies, but in the intentional choice of serving a purpose greater than profits bolstered by the commitment of passing the company baton to the next generation of leaders. "Don't drop the baton" is very different thinking from "if it hits the ground, I'll just run a different race." Endurance takes values beyond consumption, and beyond money.

We began this examination in Chapter 1 with a review of the accelerating rate of change. Those who cannot see the case for change will not endure. Stagnant, and even slow acceptance of and reaction to changing requirements, are not options. Only the rarest of those will see the next decade. Simply knowing that the same old, same old will not suffice is hardly sufficient. Living a commitment to organizational evolution in every breath you take is a good start.

Movie character Gordon Gekko told us that greed is good. I beg to differ. Greed is not the motivator that will underlie a manufacturing business that stands the test of time. There are motivations that can. Your mission, vision, and core values can earn the devotion of all constituencies when supported by the provision of value the customer appreciates. The size of your bank account cannot.

But obviously good intentions alone do not assure a long future, or any future at all.

The abilities to be comfortable with ambiguity, to distinguish the important from the merely new, to invest in developing the enterprise capabilities that can facilitate movement toward your mission, and to take nothing for granted are rare, but do not need to be. Recognizing the importance of each is, again, a good start. People can learn, and they can develop new skills and thinking. They will let go of the past when there is a reason to move toward the future. Even those outside your organization, but living in the microclimate that your business nourishes, will make changes important to your future when reasoning is clear.

The specific competencies that your organization must master will evolve over time. Interacting with those committed to learning and evolving themselves is so important. The technology, or skill, or piece of knowledge, or material that is integral to your current competencies will fade away. The one competency that will underlie your future is that of recognizing and adapting the capabilities that tomorrow requires. That competency must be a process, not a hope or dream. Random acts of observation, of learning, of changing do not light the path.

Endurance requires customers. Customers are people. People have needs and wants, some of which are physical, some emotional, some intellectual. Those needs and wants evolve over time. Because the socioeconomic environment of any business is constantly changing, so, too, must its approach to creating, recognizing, and fulfilling market demands. Capabilities must continuously improve. Not just any capability, but those that are integral to providing value to each constituency.

All five of your constituencies comprise people—human beings. They all have individual needs and wants. Those, too, evolve. Too many businesses now concentrate on developing a minimum viable product (MVP), while overlooking other critical aspects of the organization. As the leader, it is your responsibility to ensure that every aspect of the business is viable—at least minimally for today. That standard is hardly sufficient for an enduring future, but again, it is a start.

No business can survive without people. No business can survive without relationships with all constituencies. Building a successful and enduring manufacturing business always requires an understanding of and caring about people. Relationships with your constituencies will evolve and should do so intentionally. Prioritizing planned changes to any and all of those associations requires an understanding of current relationships.

The aspects of your business just summarized are not optional; neither is strategic thinking to guide the actual development and provision of value. Business schools often spend semesters teaching strategy, but little time on what enables it to matter. Choosing the direction your organization will take cannot be a random act of genius. That path cannot be internalized nor implemented without coherent, multidirectional communication. Neither abdication nor delegation without the discipline of regular follow-up are superior to aimless change.

Devotion to developing strategic thinking skills throughout the organization and providing line-of-sight clarity between tactics and strategy is another requirement of building an enduring manufacturing business. Not everyone will be a great conceptual thinker, but everyone can become aware of thinking patterns and limitations, and work to improve. Even the most linear thinker seeks to understand. When I'm exhausted, just tell me what to do. Otherwise, I want to understand why.

Each of us has felt the frustration of how much time a simple request can take to answer. A company blinded by its own self-induced obstacles will be unable to become adept at rapid, valuable change. We become better not by seeing the shining city on the hill, but by seeing how far we are from it. The ability to grasp reality, sometimes swallow hard, and then begin the trek is another enterprise capability to be mastered.

Imagine if your prior employers had cared deeply about you as a human. If they had had a purpose that excited you. If they had freely acknowledged errors and omissions and worked to prevent them in the future. If they had been proud of what *is*, but energized by what *could be*. If they had kept a finger on the pulse of the evolving future and wanted to be part of shaping it. If their commitment to flexibility and agility had enabled you to try, test, learn, share, and grow. If making the world a better place had been your reality of going to work every day, whether "go to work" meant move to your home office, become an ex-pat leader in a different part of the world, or walk to the same building day after day.

The needs and wants of these crazy younger generations are not so crazy after all. They are amazingly similar to what we would have loved to experience but didn't have the ability to consider possible. There is a way. There is always a way. The question is whether we are willing and able to develop it and take the actions and make the thinking changes required to execute it.

One of the lasting challenges of an enduring business is retaining the commitment. Understanding what truly drives your manufacturing business and never taking your eye off that ball is the mark of a strong leader. Enduring companies rely on a series of strong leaders with that same focus. It can all be ended by one leader who chooses the immediate gratification of spending money earned by a company that was built by someone else, over the satisfaction of handing over the reins closer to accomplishing the mission than the business was when that leader took over. That fragility could be depressing. Instead, prevent it by building an organization that values mission, vision, and core values over the ego of any crack in the leadership armor. It is much easier to remove a parasite, even if that parasite is your child, than to watch the demise of a living organism that provides nutrients to so many.

The soul of the enduring organization must be vibrant and thorough. The fundamental leadership principles that make the manufacturer special cannot be ignored in tough times or transition. By creating an organization that builds in human development continuity of those values is facilitated by the succession planning that naturally evolves.

You can create a virtuous cycle of change. In doing so, you will be carrying the baton carefully as you speed your manufacturing business past others. And when you're ready to hand it to the next person, that person's hand will be outstretched as they move at your pace to affect a smooth handoff.

Each of you is in a different place personally, as are your organizations. This path indicates sequence, but you will each determine your own. All of you should start with grasping current reality, gaining clarity on the future you want to create, and realistically viewing the gaps. Figure 10.1

A I say... B Our Leadership Team says...	Describes Me and Our Business					
	Not At All			Frequently		Bingo!
	0	1	2	3	4	5
Ready and Willing						
I want to and will commit to building an enduring manufacturing company						
I want to and will do the work required of me personally						
I want to and will invest personal and organizational time, energy, and other resources to build an enduring manufacturing business						
I want to and will prepare the organization for the next person to take the baton, and only pass it to someone who wants to do the same						
Financially Able						
The business is designed to be profitable						
Cash flow supports investing in the business continually						
We have and can maintain sufficient liquidity to support consistency						
Our current markets, products, and capabilities are viable to support needed timeframes						

1. If any of the above are 1, 2, or 3, you are not ready to begin building an enduring manufacturing business.
2. Any that are a 4 show what you need to address before moving forward.
3. If all are 5, you are ready, willing, and able!

Figure 10.1   Readliness Assessment

and the appendix are readiness assessments intended to help you execute those steps. Deciding where to begin closing the gap is likely one of the most impactful decisions you will ever make. The assessment also helps you weigh options as you begin to create an enduring manufacturing business.

Are You Ready and Willing?

As your business was founded, leaders were likely more interested in surviving a month, then a quarter, then a year, than in any conversation about endurance. No one starts a business expecting it to fail, but few plan for the really long term either. So now your company has some history and it's time to consider its future.

The future of a manufacturing business cannot be considered separately from the future of its constituents. While your organization is a legal entity, all businesses comprise people and all interactions are with people. Because those interactions have a financial component to them, it is easy to consider money, the business, and the owners as synonymous. In enduring businesses, they are not.

The company is much more than that, while in some ways less. The enduring manufacturing organization is the vehicle for making progress toward the defined mission and vision through the interdependent involvement of people. Is it more important to maximize benefit to the company, or to all five constituencies? The future of your company and the futures of all constituents are intertwined. The business must be profitable to fund the future, but why should a business exist that maximizes current profits to the detriment of others? If you can answer that, perhaps you are not committed to building an enduring business. That doesn't make you a bad person, just one more interested in money than a mission and vision that others want to help you bring to fruition.

Not everyone wants to build an enduring business. Startups are encouraged to define an exit plan as they seek initial funding. Many financial investors are more interested in taking the money and running, betting they'll win more than they'll lose over their life. But there are investors that care about making a difference for the world as they make money. They are not mutually exclusive. I would never argue that making money is a bad thing; merely that it's not the only thing. There are now investment funds that focus on businesses that prioritize social responsibility.

So, the first question you must answer, and not do so casually, is: Do you want to build an enduring manufacturing business (Figure 10.1)?

That requires different, unrelenting focus than does current profitability. You will be focused on the future, not today. You will be passionate about the mission and vision that will be the primary target until they are reached by someone—hopefully your organization. You will build a stronger team with amazing capabilities to accept the baton from you and keep running. And they the same for the next leader.

If you can make that commitment, the next question is about current financial stability. Do you need to design your business model and your business to be profitable? Too many hope for profits. The easiest way to recognize the difference is when an organization no longer needs to tightly control every financial decision within reasonable ranges. A lack of money should not stop intelligent investments; there should always be money for those. If each month is a mystery and each year a high-wire act, reexamining the basics of your business is your highest priority.

Establishing Your Baseline

If the changes required of creating an enduring business are accepted, and the financial stability to support those changes is in place, you are prepared to assess your beginning status in all key arenas. Each may range from nonexistent to world beating. There are no wins and losses now; you simply need to understand from where you begin this journey. Your initial assessments may be verified, or overturned, in the coming months as you better understand each of these major components described in this book.

As noted previously, the appendix provides an assessment to guide you through establishing your baseline. You may choose to add questions, edit, or delete a few, to make it most useful to your circumstances. If you think a category does not apply to you, be very careful. I did not write chapters for volume; every topic addressed is relevant to creating an enduring manufacturing business. I encourage you to test your responses vertically and horizontally to understand current differences in perception. Again, this is not about right or wrong. These answers can facilitate discussion and help facilitate the sharing of experiences that support opinions. If you don't agree on where you are, selecting a path to travel is chasing your tail. The assessment is also available at mfgmastery.com/assessment.

As you consider the questions, ask yourself honestly if your business would have described itself that way before reading this book. For example, the organization has to have a process orientation before it can claim processes in place and executed in any of the categories. Otherwise, you are likely considering the fact that things get done somehow to indicate a process that is followed. The company has to actively communicate and relate to an agreed-upon strategy—not just a budget—before it can claim alignment. The business mindset must have included relationships of mutual benefit with each of the five constituencies to claim selection and development processes with them.

Those examples simply describe how the current-state assessment is not intended to promote high self-scores in retrospect, but to grasp current reality. It's like cheating on a diet; you only hurt yourself. If you are skinny by virtue of genetics, you would still be healthier by living an understanding of nutrition and exercise. If your business has good relationships and healthy profits by luck, it will become more enduring when those are the result of designed intention. Luck comes in both good and bad.

What Next?

When you have general agreement on the current reality, you can consider which elements are most important for near-term development. While there is no prescribed sequence, there are some practical preconditions. It would be difficult to fully develop design capabilities extraordinaire without process orientation, respect for all constituencies, and an understanding of mission and core values. Similarly, a well-defined and lived business operating system can have a negative impact when mission, vision, and core values are not the basis, and when discipline is a dream. Asking people to think strategically when there is no identifiable strategy is fool's gold.

The better and more fun work that differentiates an enduring business from all the others is a lifelong pursuit. At least until the mission is achieved. Putting in place a one-, five-, or ten-year plan to become an enduring manufacturing business is an exercise in futility. Near-term plans that reflect priorities in enhancing endurance do make sense. Critical competencies of the lasting business include anticipating the need for change and identifying and mastering enterprise capabilities that the future will require.

By reviewing this assessment now to identify your baseline, and later as part of your strategy development and finalization process to build in priorities for progress, you choose a roadmap. Emerging leaders must understand and internalize the roadmap as they increase in influence. Every manager or executive brought in from the outside must become familiar with and accepting of your endurance thinking. As I wrote earlier, retaining the commitment to always pass the baton forward is essential.

Who is writing the next page and the next chapter for your company? Like the tides, be unrelenting as you build endurance into your manufacturing business.

Conclusion

This book has described nine major steps forming the path to building successful and enduring manufacturing businesses. None is a piece of cake. None is optional. But as you become increasingly comfortable and competent at each, the tenth step becomes easier.

Like a marathon racer, you know how to keep moving through the pain and the exhilaration. Climbing the hills is hardest the first time. Now you know when to speed up, when to take a breath, and how to leverage the competition to set new "company best" performance. You listen to coaches and observe others. You have integrated the thinking that an enduring company requires into the soul of your business. The body of the marathoner ages and performance declines. In your living organization, that does not need to happen. It's your choice.

The road you are running will change. You will find hills in new places and of seemingly steeper incline. None of that need throw you off kilter. You can rely on your training, thinking, learning experiences, and the organizational organism you have nurtured. Never losing sight of that is what can enable yours to become an evergreen company. A truly evergreen business will always have customers and strategic profits, and someday, accomplish its mission.

THE EVERGREEN MANUFACTURER: FINAL THOUGHTS

■ One of the lasting challenges of an enduring business is retaining the commitment to passing the baton of a healthy company.

■ Businesses that endure focus on ensuring the future, not on building a bigger today. Perhaps that distinction is why so few manufacturing businesses do stand the test of time.

- The one competency that will underlie your future is that of recognizing and adapting the capabilities that tomorrow requires. That competency must be a process, not a hope or dream.

Making more and more money may please you, but the rest of the world really doesn't care about that. Continually delivering increasing value as the mission and vision become ever closer gains the active support of all your constituencies. Some people search for meaning; others create meaning by building a successful and enduring manufacturing business.

Appendix

		Describes Me and Our Business					
		Not At All			Frequently		Bingo!
(A) I say...		0	1	2	3	4	5
(B) Our Leadership Team says...							
(C) Our Employees say...							
(D) Our Other 4 Constituencies say...							
Need for Change							
We understand and live the constant need for change to benefit all of our constituencies							
Mission, Vision, Core Values							
I believe in and am committed to the company mission and vision, which accurately reflect our *why* and our *what*							
I believe in and will behave in line with our defined core values, which are consistent with our mission and vision							
Our mission, vision, and core values attract constituencies integral to building an enduring company							
Enterprise Capabilities							
Our culture and leadership behaviors reflect a healthy and well-understood business operating system							
We are continually committed to and active in developing our employees and business partners							
We recognize the importance of effective design to all aspects of our business							
Designing all aspects of our business is a strong competency							
Our true competitive advantage is in our mastery of thinking, integrating, and value-adding							
We constantly work to better integrate speed, quality, and cost considerations into our systems and processes as we focus on becoming more agile, resilient, and responsive							
Ambiguity is a source of opportunity, not something to fear							

Figure A.1   Readiness Assessment: Establishing Your Baseline

	Describes Me and Our Business					
Ⓐ I say... Ⓑ Our Leadership Team says... Ⓒ Our Employees say... Ⓓ Our Other 4 Constituents say...	Not At All			Frequently		Bingo!
	0	1	2	3	4	5
Relationships						
We care about and continually strive to benefit all five of our constituencies						
Our processes that define selection, development, and evaluation of each constituent group and the individual members specifically incorporate intended mutual benefit						
We build improving constituent relationships into our strategies						
The markets we will serve see us as integral to their futures						
We understand that whether considering quality, speed, and cost attributes, or competencies reflected in agility, resilience, and responsiveness, all constituents impact our reality						
We intentionally identify and maximize constituent contribution to our success and accept the responsibility to help them help us						
Strategy Development and Finalization						
We understand that strategy defines "how" we will move forward with our *what* to achieve our *why*						
We have an effective strategy development and finalization methodology that builds in vertical and horizontal feedback, prioritization, and visibility						
The content of our strategies is the vehicle to create agility, responsiveness, and other capabilities we believe integral to success within the cost, speed, and quality parameters specified in its design						
Our strategies reflect the most effective alternatives in making progress toward our mission and vision						
Our strategy is a living thing, anchoring priorities and decisions, reviewed constantly, and updated as needed						

Figure A.1   (Continued)

		Describes Me and Our Business					
A I say...		Not At All			Frequently		Bingo!
B Our Leadership Team says...							
C Our Employees say...		0	1	2	3	4	5
D Our Other 4 Constituents say...							
Strategy Deployment							
Our business operating system builds in tight multi-directional connectedness of tactics to strategy							
We understand that organizational alignment results from effective strategy deployment that builds in multi-directional communication							
We build in continuous line of sight to top strategic objectives for all employees							
We understand that budget reflects strategy, but is certainly not strategy							
Tactical and Strategic Thinking							
We do not let standard costing or the cost-center mentality constrain potential contributions of operations to business success							
Operations is responsible for customer satisfaction and retention							
Operations is responsible for knowing and anticipating market needs and wants and determining the supply mechanisms that best develop value performance for the organization							
We continually link operational decisions to strategy through our line-of-sight process to facilitate strategic thinking							

Figure A.1   (Continued)

	Describes Me and Our Business					
(A) I say... **(B)** Our Leadership Team says... **(C)** Our Employees say... **(D)** Our Other 4 Constituents say...	Not At All			Frequently		Bingo!
	0	1	2	3	4	5
Overcoming Obstacles						
We do not and we will not accept low expectations AND accept responsibility for processes and systems that support high expectations						
We always tie priorities to the strategy and will not walk away from our responsibility to ensure clear priorities supported by resource allocation						
We are committed to providing information where and when it is needed to support fast, effective decision-making throughout the organization						
We accept that leaders provide the rules, tools, and conditions for constituent success in supporting our organization						
Confusion on priorities and status is typically the result of ineffective leadership communication and discipline						
We demonstrate that perseverance does not imply a lack of trust; it implies significance						
We validate all metrics as useful in improving the quality of decisions, or in informing constituents of results						
We distinguish between lead indicators that drive decisions and lagging indicators that reflect results						
Organizational Structure						
Our current organizational structure reflects a conscious decision						
Our structure simplifies and facilitates strategy implementation						
Our structure builds in operating system and strategic objectives						
Constituents fully understand how our current structure works and are free to suggest improvements and point out weaknesses						

Figure A.1   (Continued)

	Describes Me and Our Business					
A I say... **B** Our Leadership Team says... **C** Our Employees say... **D** Our Other 4 Constituents say...	Not At All			Frequently		Bingo!
	0	1	2	3	4	5
Evergreen						
We understand that financial growth is not the primary objective						
We understand that personal, relationship, value, and capabilities growth propel us toward our mission and vision						
We are focused on building a better future, not on building a bigger today						
We are continually committed to passing the baton of a healthy, worthwhile, and mission-driven manufacturing business						
We believe that a truly evergreen business will always have customers and strategic profits, and someday, accomplish its mission						

Figure A.1   (Continued)

Glossary

after-action report (AAR): Best known for its use by the military, and sometimes referred to as a postmortem, this is an after-the-fact analysis of the response of leadership and systems to an event. The purpose is to identify what went well, what did not, and to create changes that will ensure better future responses. These are also performed upon completion of major projects.

artificial intelligence (AI): Artificial intelligence generically refers to machines performing cognitive functions. Technologies included or excluded in AI definitions change over time. For example, optical character recognition (OCR) is now commonplace and no longer considered an AI technology, while autonomous driving is included in most lists of AI capabilities.

B Lab: A nonprofit, international organization that certifies organizations as meeting "the highest standards of verified social and environmental performance, public transparency, and legal accountability to balance profit and purpose." The certification process reviews the entire business, far beyond products and services, and requires commitment to ongoing actions to maintain those standards.

business operating system (BOS): The combination of culture and processes that define, but more importantly demonstrate, for an organization "how we think and act." It reflects relationships, assumptions, priorities, and, to some degree, methodology, while reflecting core values, mission, and vision.

CRISPR: An acronym for clustered, regularly interspaced, short palindromic repeats, it is a technology of gene sequencing and DNA modification integral to much state-of-the-art health care.

constituencies: The individuals and groups that an organization interacts with and impacts. Categories are investors, customers/markets, suppliers, employees, and the community at large, which includes the future.

community at large: One of the constituencies of a manufacturing business, it includes not only the immediate physical neighborhood, but all peoples and parts of the world impacted by its business practices. Because of scarce resources and shared natural resources, this includes the future as well.

Delusional Excellence®: A "condition" in which an organization views itself as much better than facts support. Frequently it results from spotlighting progress on internal operational goals. It may reflect inadequate knowledge of what the best are doing, sometimes due to limited arenas considered (e.g., only basic production statistics), and sometimes due to unverifiable assumptions. It is differentiated from true excellence.

factory-as-a-service (FaaS): As agility, flexibility, and speed become increasingly important to manufacturers, the time and cost of building a capital-intensive operation to pilot a new concept, test a market, or even run varying production volumes, is high risk. FaaS is a production environment, often facilitated by smart factory technologies, in which capacity and setup are sold to run production on the equipment of a FaaS company. These are often capable of much, optimized for little, but as smart support continues to grow, will improve even further.

Factory Physics: A book written by Wallace Hopp and Mark Spearman, now in its third edition and with supporting materials. It explains data-driven, rules-based operations flow mathematics and thinking. The concepts and mathematical realities are applicable far beyond the factory floor.

Finish Strong®: A business concept trademarked by author Rebecca Morgan that answers the question Given that you and your competitors are each likely to be skilled at the technical side of your business, how can you routinely and consistently execute better than they?

holacracy: A theory of management that alleges to facilitate agility and flexibility of purpose-driven companies by foregoing official roles and most reporting structures. Individuals are expected to self-organize into work groups to address issues and opportunities, with the group dispersing after the issue is resolved.

Industry 4.0: This phrase is considered synonymous with the "fourth industrial revolution." It refers generally to the expanding use of data and technology in all manufacturing industries. While originally limited to production, evolution has shown Industry 4.0 capabilities value-adding throughout businesses and supply chains. As technologies advance and we learn more about what works and what does not, the specifics of what is included and what is not evolves.

location-independence: The growing customer expectation that they will receive the product or service where they want to, not simply at manufacturer-defined locations. In services it is easy to see this in action by considering Sirius® radios, which allow favorite audio entertainment services to travel seamlessly. In goods it is primarily being handled by shippers like UPS and Fed-EX now, which offer the recipient freedom to change or specify an atypical location. Carvana is an automotive sales example.

microclimate: Generally, this refers to the climate in a small area that is different from surrounding areas. For purposes of this book, it refers to the manufacturer and its five constituencies, which can have very different realities than other businesses in the area or in the industry.

minimum viable product (MVP): This concept is intended to speed effective product development by testing an offering with early adopters to receive feedback and enter the market before additional value is added to it. That learning is used to continue development for the greater market. The focus is more on market acceptance than on other aspects of design.

mission: The reason *why* a manufacturing business exists. Decisions and actions are chosen to provide consistency and move the company closer to accomplishing its mission.

Moore's Law: The public observations of Gordon Moore that lowering computing costs had been enabled by increasing the number of transistors on computer chips for several years were converted into the eponymous law the number of transistors per chip would continue to double every year, cutting computing costs by 50 percent as a result. The law was revised in the mid-1970s to every two years, and now the law's natural end has been pronounced by many, rejected by some.

operational health: Differentiated from organizational health but interdependent, this concept focuses on the capabilities of the operations aspects of a manufacturing business. Operational competencies that stand apart from the crowd demand a combination of well-designed processes and people continually learning, augmented by appropriate technology. It is not defined by product or by shop-floor metrics. It is assessed by reliable provision of profitable value to the markets, consistent with mission, vision, and core values. Manufacturers with healthy operations can advance powerful competitive advantage in understanding and surpassing the needs of all constituents.

operations technology (OT): Distinct from information technology (IT) and product technology (PT), this refers to the technologies utilized as part of Industry 4.0 in operational functions. The management of these three technology applications is rarely effectively assigned to one IT leader, but rather is executed by coordinated responsibilities and decision-making by the experts in each arena.

organizational health: Differentiated from operational health but interdependent, this term focuses on the capabilities of the entire business, including relationships with all constituencies. It reflects targeted organizational characteristics developed and sustained by a business operating system that frames "this is how we think and act." Additionally, a high level of organizational health requires unwavering development of people and a focus on design throughout the microclimate. A sufficient level of organizational health is a prerequisite to operational health.

product technology (PT): Distinct from information technology (IT) and operations technology (OT), this refers to the technologies utilized in the products themselves to collect data and enable new servicing and service offerings. The management of these three technologies is rarely effectively assigned to one IT leader, but rather is executed by coordinated responsibilities and decision-making by the experts in each arena. This cannot be left solely to product management responsibilities, but their involvement is important.

product-as-a-service (PaaS): This is a change in business model for most manufacturers, as rather than sell the product, the company sells the benefits and outcomes the product can provide. It typically reflects a change in traditional asset ownership and is a common component of organizations that focus on the circular economy.

purpose: Mission is the reason *why* your business exists. Vision is a description of *what* that will entail as it is accomplished. Core values are the truths that your business will live by in the entirety of its behavior. Strategy is the chosen path—the *how*—to fulfill the vision. Purpose is the foundation for all.

robotic process automation (RPA): A technical capability—a software product—that enables simple and relatively easy automation of repeated, rules-based tasks, replacing that drudgery of human work with automation.

social responsibility of business: In the second half of the twentieth century, this was considered an oxymoron, but has since become a generally accepted role for publicly held, for-profit manufacturers. This is hand-in-glove with the reduction of focus on maximizing profits for the sole benefit of stockholders and the increased emphasis on considering the well-being of all five constituencies in business decisions. The medical oath of "first do no harm" is being applied to business, with the concept of *harm* including investors, customers/markets, suppliers, employees, and importantly, the community at large, which includes the future.

strategic profits: Strategic profits are those built and utilized through design and operation of the business to fund an enduring company so that it can better reach its mission and vision, in alignment with its core values. Some companies make strategic profit decisions, and others simply make decisions that impact profits.

strategy: The *prioritized how* an organization will execute to move forward, at least near term, toward its vision and mission.

supply chain total costs (SCTC): Total cost of ownership (TCO) considers a broader range of costs to the buying company than does purchase price. SCTC looks beyond TOC and the view of a single manufacturer and considers the total supply chain when evaluating cost reduction alternatives. It recognizes that supply chains now compete with other supply chains and that shifting costs from one organization to another changes individual performance results, but does little—if anything—to reduce total costs.

technical debt: Typically considering software, technical debt refers to built-in rework from taking shortcuts to meet a target date. It reflects a choice of speed over quality in software development. The concept can apply more broadly to product development and implementation of IIoT technologies from making comparable choices that knowingly necessitate later rework.

total cost of ownership (TCO): The purchase price of an item used by a manufacturer is only one part of the total costs related to that item. Looking from the viewpoint of the manufacturer, TCO also includes handling, inspecting, and other costs associated with acquiring and preparing that item for use in the value-add manufacturing process. This concept has the impact of purchasing evaluating and making decisions, considering other item-related costs than merely the purchase order price.

true excellence: Improving the accomplishment of vision and mission in ways that excite all five constituencies investors, customers/markets, suppliers, employees, and the community at large. It requires a purpose higher than profits, increasing benefit to all constituencies, and a passion for both.

Truly Human Leadership: The name that Bob Chapman and Barry-Wehmiller have given their specific approach to a people-centric leadership philosophy. In all interactions the company is expected to emphasize the full human that is more than just the employee paid for their work.

user-controlled pull: The growing customer expectation that they can choose when to utilize a product or service rather than be subject to the provider's supply schedule. Streaming services are one example, giving new meaning to the term *binging*. The responsiveness of Amazon has reinforced that expectation, such that an order promise date other than today has become less acceptable.

virtual/assisted/augmented/mixed reality (VR/AR/MR): Each of these refers to the use of visioning technologies to help people see what they otherwise could not. **Virtual reality** refers to a completely computer-generated, three-dimensional view that the individual can interact with by means of sensors or other devices. Many popular games and planning new factories are examples of current applications. **Assisted reality** is the ability to see a screen right in front of the person, hands-free. A car projecting current speed on the inside of the driver's windshield is one example. **Augmented reality** allows the individual to use multiple senses, although almost always vision, to see a combination of data or other virtual enhancements superimposed on the real world. A wiring diagram superimposed on the piece of equipment maintenance is actually looking at is a common example. **Mixed reality** is a combination of virtual and physical reality in which the individual can manipulate virtual, to-scale holograms among actual items in place. The Microsoft HoloLens® is a common tool in the market today. There are numerous practical applications, from training to floor layout to remote work.

vision: *What* (high-level path) a manufacturer will emphasize in accomplishing its mission. It describes a recognizable next state for progress. It is often determined by the expertise of the business founder. For an example, refer to Chapter 5.

References

3M. "3M Accelerates Pace of Transformation Journey." January 2020. https://news
.3m.com/English/press-releases/press-releases-details/2020/3M-Accelerates
-Pace-of-Transformation-Journey/default.aspx.

Akao, Yoji. *Hoshin Kanri: Policy Deployment for Successful TQM.* New York:
Productivity Press, 2004.

Allworth, James. "The 787's Problems Run Deeper than Outsourcing." *Harvard
Business Review*, January 30, 2013. https://hbr.org/2013/01/the-787s-problems
-run-deeper-t.

Alzheimer's Association. "About." Accessed October 30, 2020. https://www.alz.org/
about.

Barry-Wehmiller. "Truly Human Leadership." Accessed December 6, 2020. https://
trulyhumanleadership.com/?p=633.

Brock, David C. *Understanding Moore's Law.* Philadelphia: Chemical Heritage Press,
2006.

Business Roundtable. "Business Roundtable Redefines the Purpose of a Corporation
to Promote 'An Economy That Serves All Americans.'" Accessed August 19,
2019. https://www.businessroundtable.org/business-roundtable-redefines-the-p
urpose-of-a-corporation-to-promote-an-economy-that-serves-all-americans.

Cambridge Air Solutions, Inc. "Helping Leaders in Manufacturing and Warehousing
Create Healthy Working Environments for Hard-Working People." Accessed
September 19, 2020. https://www.cambridgeair.com/.

Carpenter Wellington PLLC. "B Corps vs. Benefit Corporations: Understanding the
Key Distinctions." Accessed August 11, 2020. https://carpenterwellington.com/
post/b-corps-vs-benefit-corporations-the-key-distinctions/.

Chapman, Bob, and Rajendra Sisodia. *Everybody Matters.* New York: Penguin, 2015.

Choudhury, Amit Roy, and Jim Mortleman. "How IoT Is Turning Rolls-Royce into a
Data-Fuelled Business." *I: Global Intelligence for Digital Leaders.* January 2018.
https://www.i-cio.com/innovation/internet-of-things/item/how-iot-is-turning
-rolls-royce-into-a-data-fuelled-business.

Christensen, Clayton M. *The Innovator's Dilemma.* Boston: Harvard Business
Review Press, 1997.

Cipresso, Pietro, Irene Giglioli, Alice Chicchi, Mariano Raya, and Giuseppe Riva. "The Past, Present, and Future of VR and AR." *Frontiers in Psychology*, November 2018.

Cole, Robert E. "What Really Happened to Toyota?" *MIT Sloan Management Review*, June 22, 2011.

Cornell Law School. "Common Misunderstandings about Corporations." Accessed September 2, 2020. https://www.lawschool.cornell.edu/academics/clarke_business_law:institute/corporations-and-society/Common-Misunderstandings-About-Corporations.cfm.

Crosby, Philip B. *Quality is Free: The Art of Making Quality Certain*. New York: McGraw-Hill, 1979.

Davies, Rob. "How Unilever Foiled Kraft Heinz's £115bn Takeover Bid." *The Guardian*, US Edition, February 20, 2017. https://www.theguardian.com/business/2017/feb/20/how-unilever-foiled-kraft-heinzs-115m-takeover-bid-warren-buffett.

Deming, William Edwards. *The New Economics: For Industry, Government, Education*. Cambridge, MA: MIT Press, 2000.

Dooley, Ben, and Hisako Ueno. "This Japanese Shop Is 1,020 Years Old. It Knows a Bit about Surviving Crises." *The New York Times*. December 2, 2020. https://www.nytimes.com/2020/12/02/business/japan-old-companies.html?campaign_id=9&emc=edit_nn_20201202&instance_id=24634&nl=the-morning&regi_id=58584194&segment_id=45848&te=1&user_id=d5c842d04aa8072a3fe0e6996e980cfc.

Dorsey, Jason R., and Denise Villa. *Zconomy*. New York: HarperBusiness, 2020.

Drucker, Peter F. *The Practice of Management*. New York: HarperBusiness, 1993.

Friedman, Milton. "A Friedman Doctrine: The Social Responsibility of Business Is to Increase Its Profits." *The New York Times Magazine*, September 13, 1970. https://www.nytimes.com/1970/09/13/archives/a-friedman-doctrine-the-social-responsibility-of-business-is-to.html.

Friedman, Milton. *Capitalism and Freedom*, 40th Anniversary Edition. Chicago: University of Chicago Press, 2002.

George, William W., and Amram Migdal. *Battle for the Soul of Capitalism: Unilever and the Kraft Heinz Takeover Bid (A)*. Boston: Harvard Business School Case 317–127, May 2017. https://store.hbr.org/product/battle-for-the-soul-of-capitalism-unilever-and-the-kraft-heinz-takeover-bid-a/317127.

Google. "Our Approach to Search." Accessed October 30, 2020. https://www.google.com/search/howsearchworks/mission/.

Groth, Aimee. "Zappos Has Quietly Backed Away from Holacracy." *Quartz at Work*, January 29, 2020. https://qz.com/work/1776841/zappos-has-quietly-backed-away-from-holacracy/.

Heath, Chip, and Dan Heath. *Decisive*. New York: Crown Business, 2013.

Industrial Scientific. "About Us." Accessed September 6, 2020. https://www.indsci.com/en/about-us/.

Mackey, John, and Raj Sisodia. *Conscious Capitalism*. Boston: Harvard Business School Publishing, 2014.

Mann, David. *Creating a Lean Culture*, 3rd Edition. New York: Productivity Press, 2014.

Marples, Donald J., and Jane G. Gravelle. *Corporate Expatriation, Inversions, and Mergers: Tax Issues*. Congressional Research Service, 2019. https://fas.org/sgp/crs/misc/R43568.pdf.

McClenahen, John. "The Book on the One-Day Close." *IndustryWeek*, December 21, 2004. https://www.industryweek.com/finance/software-systems/article/21948670/the-book-on-the-oneday-close.

Mishel, Lawrence, and Jori Kandra. "CEO Compensation Surged 14% in 2019 to $21.3 Million: CEOs Now Earn 320 Times as Much as a Typical Worker." *Economic Policy Institute*, August 18, 2020. https://www.epi.org/publication/ceo-compensation-surged-14-in-2019-to-21-3-million-ceos-now-earn-320-times-as-much-as-a-typical-worker/.

Monks, Robert A. G., and Nell Minow. *Corporate Governance*, 4th Edition. West Sussex, UK: Wiley, 2008.

Nader, Ralph. *Unsafe at Any Speed*. New York: Grossman Publishers, 1995.

Nasdaq, RTTNews. "3M Announces New Global Operating Model; to Cut about 1,500 Jobs: Quick Facts." January 28, 2020. https://www.nasdaq.com/articles/3m-announces-new-global-operating-model-to-cut-about-1500-jobs-quick-facts-2020-01-28.

Parry, Charles, and Marilyn Darling. "Emergent Learning in Action: The After Action Review." *The Systems Thinker*. Accessed September 2, 2020. https://thesystemsthinker.com/emergent-learning-in-action-the-after-action-review/.

Podolny, Joel M., and Morten T. Hansen. "How Apple Is Organized for Innovation." *Harvard Business Review*, November–December 2020.

Ritchie, Hannah, and Max Roser. "Age Structure." *Our World in Data*, September 2019. https://ourworldindata.org/age-structure.

Rosenfield, Donald B., and Steve Eppinger. "Will Risk Result in Reward for Boeing's Dreamliner?" *MIT Sloan Executive Education*, July 11, 2013. https://executive.mit.edu/blog/will-risk-result-in-reward-for-boeings-dreamliner.

Salary.com. "Why Do CEOs Make the Big Bucks?" Accessed December 2, 2020. https://www.salary.com/articles/why-do-ceos-make-the-big-bucks/.

Spear, Stephen J. *The High-Velocity Edge*, 2nd Edition. New York: McGraw-Hill Education, 2010.

Statista. "Ratio Between CEO and Average Worker Pay in 2018, By Country." Accessed December 2, 2020. https://www.statista.com/statistics/424159/pay-gap-between-ceos-and-average-workers-in-world-by-country/.

Stewart, Thomas A., and Anand P. Raman. "Lessons from Toyota's Long Drive." *Harvard Business Review*, July–August 2007.

Tesla. "About Tesla." Accessed October 30, 2020. https://www.tesla.com/about.

Toyota Motor Corporation. "Akio Toyoda's View on Toyota Production System." *Toyota Times*, August 26, 2020. https://toyotatimes.jp/en/insidetoyota/091.html.

Toyota Motor Corporation. "Toyota Global Vision." Accessed October 30, 2020. https://global.toyota/en/company/vision-and-philosophy/global-vision/.

Unilever. "About Unilever." Accessed September 4, 2020. https://www.unilever.com/about/who-we-are/about-Unilever/.

Unilever. "Our history." Accessed December 6, 2020. https://www.unilever.com/about/who-we-are/our-history/#timeline+2D+none+closed.

U.S. Minnesota Law Review. *A Legal Theory of Shareholder Primacy*, edited by Robert J Rhee. Minnesota, 2018. https://www.minnesotalawreview.org/wp-content/uploads/2018/06/Rhee_MLR.pdf.

Walker, Jennie. "How to Reconnect Teams with Your Mission, Vision & Values." In *Inside HR*, Digital Edition. January 13, 2017. https://www.researchgate.net/publication/329584615_Walker_JL_January_2017_How_to_reconnect_teams_with_your_mission_vision_values_Inside_HR_digital_edition.

Wikipedia. "Wikipedia: Purpose." Accessed October 30, 2020. https://en.wikipedia.org/wiki/Wikipedia:Purpose.

Womack, James P., Daniel T. Jones, and Daniel Roos. *The Machine That Changed the World*, New York: Simon & Schuster, 1990.

Index

Printed in the United States
by Baker & Taylor Publisher Services